LEAVINGS

A Canadian Love Story

Dear Bev,
I didn't know it at the time, but the editing of this book would lead me down the path of the exploits of my grandfather, Billy Christmas.
Love,
Girray Christmas
9/22/2015

LEAVINGS
A Canadian Love Story

William Richard Christmas

Transcribed & Edited

By

Girard Richard Christmas

Lulu Enterprises
Raleigh, North Carolina
2011

Copyrighted 2011 by Girard Richard Christmas

All Rights Reserved

No part of this book may be reproduced or transmitted in any form or by any means, graphic, electronic, or mechanical, including photocopying, recording, taping, or by any informational storage retrieval system, without the permission in writing from the editor (named above) or publisher, except by a reviewer who may quote brief passages in a review to be printed in a newspaper or magazine.

Trade paperback edition published 2011.
Published by Lulu Enterprises, Inc., Raleigh, North Carolina

For information, contact
gerry.christmas@gmail.com

ISBN: 978-1-257-10111-5

Printed in the United States of America
First Edition

Book design by Girard Richard Christmas

Cover photograph: Madeleine and Marcelle Hudon (a.k.a. "the Twins") at the time of their employment at the Sun Life Assurance Company of Montréal (circa 1930).
Christmas Family Collection

To my sons

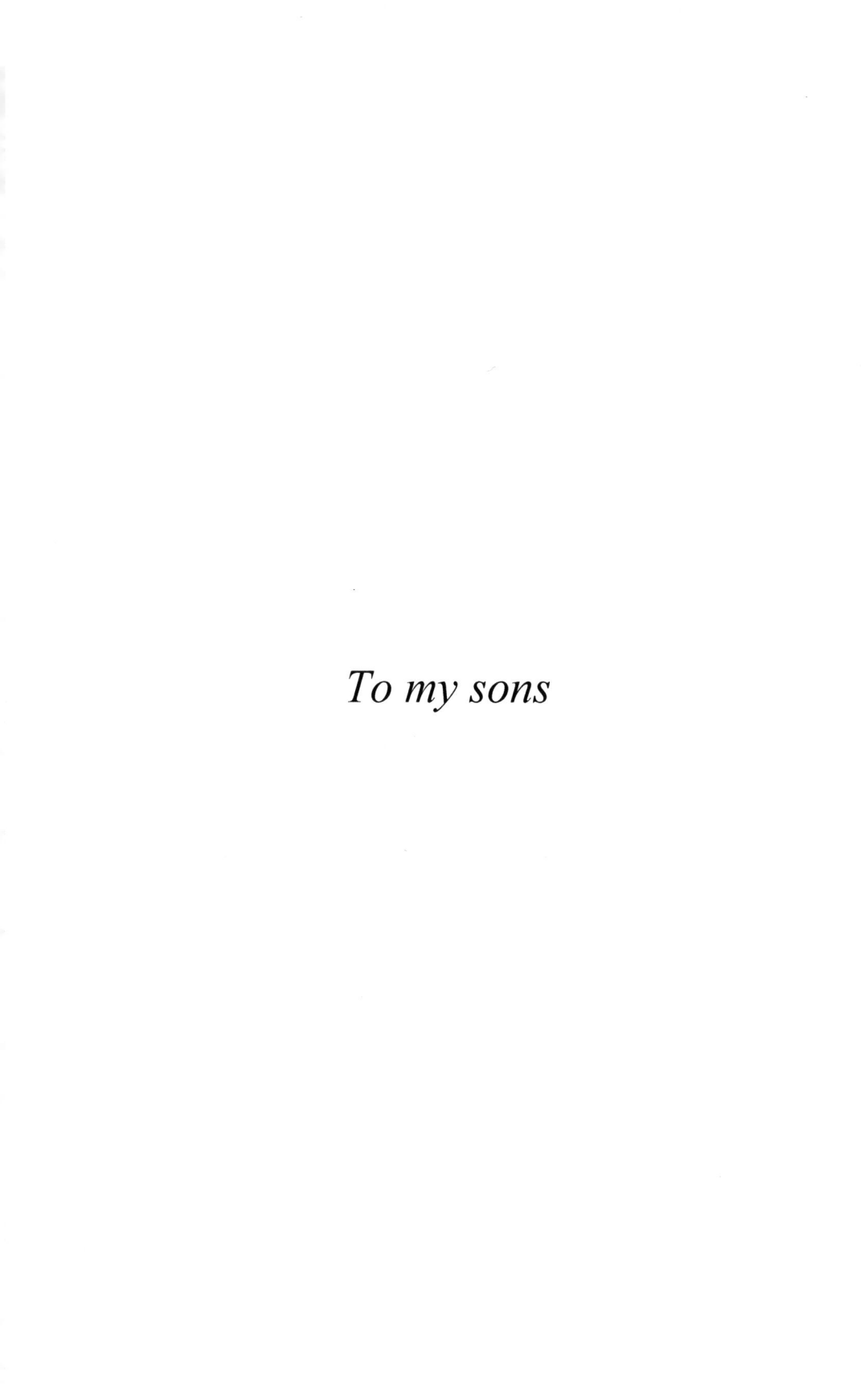

In regione caecorum rex est luscus.
Au pays des aveugles le borgne est roi.
In the land of the blind the one-eyed man is king.

>Desiderius Eramus
>*Adagia* (III, IV, 96)

I will have none of my sister's leavings.

>Marcelle Hudon to Dick Christmas

CONTENTS

INTRODUCTION xiii
BILLET-DOUX xvii
A Love Letter xvii
AVANT-PROPOS xix
Preface xix

PART ONE: MONTREAL

CHAPTER 1:	COMPAGNON DE VOYAGE 3
	Traveling Companion 3
CHAPTER 2:	EMBARRAS DE RICHESSES 7
	Embarrassing Surplus of Riches 7
CHAPTER 3:	SANS SOUCI 11
	Without Worry 11
CHAPTER 4:	DE MAL EN PIS 15
	From Bad to Worse 15
CHAPTER 5:	AU PAYS DES AVEUGLES LE BORGNE EST ROI 17
	In the Land of the Blind the One-eyed Man Is King 17
CHAPTER 6:	MAUVAISE HOUTE 21
	Bashfulness 21
CHAPTER 7:	A BON CHAT, BON RAT 25
	To a Good Cat, a Good Rat 25
CHAPTER 8:	EN FAMILLE 33
	With One's Family 33
CHAPTER 9:	ENFANT GATE 39
	Spoiled Child 39
CHAPTER 10:	ANCIENNE NOBLESSE 41
	Old-time Nobility 41
CHAPTER 11:	ALEA JUCTA EST 43
	The Die Is Cast 43

CHAPTER 12:	FEUX D'ARTIFICE	47
	Fireworks	*47*
CHAPTER 13:	J'ACCUSE	51
	I Accuse	*51*
CHAPTER 14:	PEU A PEU	55
	Little by Little	*55*
CHAPTER 15:	LE BELLE DAME SANS MERCI	59
	The Beautiful Lady Without Mercy	*59*
CHAPTER 16:	PIECE JUSTIFICATIVE	65
	Justificatory Paper	*65*
CHAPTER 17:	EN AMI	73
	As a Friend	*73*
CHAPTER 18:	AU MIEUX	77
	On Intimate terms	*77*
CHAPTER 19:	GUERRE A OUTRANCE	81
	War to the Uttermost	*81*

PART TWO: SPRINGFIELD

CHAPTER 20:	A BRAS OUVERTS	89
	With Open Arms	*89*
CHAPTER 21:	BEAU GESTE	93
	A Magnanimous Gesture	*93*

PART THREE: BOSTON

CHAPTER 22:	MAL VU	99
	Badly Regarded	*99*
CHAPTER 23:	PEINE FORTE ET DURE	101
	Strong and Harsh Punishment	*101*

PART FOUR: JACKSONVILLE

CHAPTER 24:	COUTE QUE COUTE	105
	Cost What It May	*105*
CHAPTER 25:	VA ET VIENT	107
	Coming and Going	*107*

PART FIVE: VERMONT

CHAPTER 26: EN RETRAITE..111
In Retirement 111

PART SIX: ORLANDO

CHAPTER 27: LE COEUR A SES RAISONS QUE LA
RAISON NE CONNAIT POINT............................117
*The Heart Has Its Reasons That Reason Knows
Nothing Of 117*

INTRODUCTION

My father died on March 12, 1997, just a few months shy of his ninetieth birthday. Recently while going through his personal effects I found an unfinished seventy-page letter detailing the highpoints of his life. Addressed to my brother and me, the letter was most curious. The first twenty pages were in chronological order and read quite easily. The last fifty did not. They jumped around in time with often two or three versions of the same event. In a word the manuscript was a muddle.

I honestly did not know if my father's "letter" was salvageable, if it could be edited into one coherent whole. Still, I decided to try. The major changes to the original text are as follows:

- The Preface now contains information on the Christmas family, something my father failed to include. I added this for balance. My father only had information on the Palmer, the Tillson, and Turk families.
- Two anecdotes on William Cecil Christmas were added: the first being a prank he played as a young man and the second being the events surrounding his death. My father related both these events to me, and I immediately wrote them down without embellishment of any kind.
- Some events are repeated two or three times. Here I had to choose the event that seemed the most logical and accurate. It was that or become redundant.
- The narrative jumps around wildly in space and time. I therefore decided to break the letter into chapters. Then I could correct the chronology and smooth out the narrative. I also put French and English titles on the chapters. This is a nod to my mother who once said to me: "Gerry, all you ever talk about is being an English Canadian. Never forget your French side. You should be proud of that too." Don't worry, Mom. I am.

- The original letter has no dialogue whatsoever. Whenever two people are talking, my father always resorted to indirect, not direct speech. This was a mistake for it slowed the narrative flow. I therefore used direct speech whenever I had a chance.

My father never intended his letter for a wide audience. Still, he would not object to family members knowing what manner of man he was. A lover of history, he most certainly would want his descendants to be aware of the obstacles he faced and, more importantly, how he met and overcame those obstacles– first in isolation then with his "one true love."

Gerry Christmas
Carrboro, North Carolina
November 2010

Dick Christmas in his naval uniform during World War II (circa 1944). By war's end he had reached the rank of lieutenant commander in the Royal Canadian Navy

Christmas Family Collection

BILLET-DOUX

A Love Letter

Dear Bill and Gerry:

Being retired as a few advantages– the most important being the leisure to contemplate life in general and my own in particular. I have spent a lot of time on this subject and have reached some unexpected conclusions. As my sons I hope you will indulge your father's final thoughts on life and living.

                                            Love,
                                            Dad

                                            Central Park Village
                                            Orlando, Florida

AVANT-PROPOS

Preface

Genealogy has never interested me much. Still, I know a few sketchy things about my people and will set them down here.

My paternal great-grandfather and great-grandmother were Thomas James Christmas and Charlotte Margaret Hardisty, respectively. They met in Montreal in the early 1850s and fell madly in love. They would subsequently have eight children– the first being my grandfather, Thomas Henry Christmas.

In 1840 my great-grandfather emigrated from England to the United States at the age of ten. I don't know much about him, except that he was trained as a hatter and furrier and came to Montreal from Troy, New York.

My great-grandmother came from a prosperous Canadian family. She was a minor at the time of her marriage, so there is some speculation about "a shotgun wedding." The marriage, however, was a long and happy one, despite great hardships and adversities.

My great-grandfather died when I was twelve and my great-grandmother followed two years later. I therefore cannot recall too many details about them. I can only remember that they were kind and gentle people. Perhaps that is enough.

While in my early twenties my father gave me a signet ring with a lion rampant and the motto *gweithred a ddengys*. Unable to read the motto, I ignored it. Still, I loved the ring. It was a perfect fit, and I wore it on my pinkie for years. Finally I passed it on to my older son Bill who in turn gave it to his younger brother Gerry. Gerry discovered that the motto came from the Ellis family in Glasfryn, Caernarvonshire, Wales, United Kingdom. When translated, the motto read "by our deeds we will be known."

This came as a great shock to me. I had always heard that we were "Devonshire Christmases." Where did this Ellis family fit in?[1] What made it doubly intriguing was that one of my great uncles was named Wynn Ellis Horace Christmas. Obviously my great-grandparents were proud of both their English and their Welsh heritages.

My mother was descended from the Turkington family on the paternal side, and the Palmer family on the maternal side.

The Palmers, a surname derived from knights returning from the Crusades with palms in medieval times, traced their ancestry back to William the Conqueror in England where they were squires.

The Palmer name was a prominent and respected one in Montreal. Wesley Palmer established the first barbershop. Later converted into a beauty parlor, it became the largest and most famous in the city. Wesley Palmer died a wealthy man.

On the maternal side of the Turkington family was the Tillson family. The Tillsons founded the town of Tillsonburg, Ontario after fleeing New England because of their Loyalist leanings (United Empire Loyalists).

Ellen Palmer was "given" by her wealthy family to the church. She married George Richard Turkington. George, an able Methodist minister of modest means, shortened his surname to Turk. He was successful at his work and was moved frequently from parish to parish, as was the custom of the day. By middle age he had seen duty in almost all major Eastern Canadian parishes and was finally sent to a parish somewhere in Georgia. This was analogous to missionary work and was not to his liking. He died alone, broken and defeated, his wife having succumbed to cancer at the age of fifty.

---

[1] It most likely derives from the maternal side via one Susannah Hardisty.

PART ONE

Montreal

2   Leavings

William Cecil "Billie" Christmas, age 19, in "Winged Wheeler" uniform of the Montréal Amateur Athletic Association (1898). Billie played on various sports teams for both the M.A.A.A. and his nearby hometown of Westmount.

Christmas Family Collection

Chapter 1

COMPAGNON DE VOYAGE

Traveling Companion

My grandfather Thomas Henry Christmas died in 1927, leaving an estate of more than one million dollars. In those days being a millionaire really meant something. He was a Montrealer by birth and had eight sons– all of whom were well regarded and lived and died in that city. None ever attended a university, which was not unusual in those days. Indeed at no time were the "boys" exposed to books of substance. Each graduated from high school without distinction. They were not hostile toward intellectuals; rather they viewed them as being unmanly and beneath their contempt. The cartoonist's depiction of the intellectual as the absent-minded professor suited the Christmases to a tee.

All eight boys were definitely athletically inclined, with my father in particular excelling in several sports. Indeed, Dad became a celebrated amateur athlete while still in his teens. At the age of sixteen he was a member of the Montreal Senior Hockey Team dubbed the "Little Men of Iron."[2] This team won the Stanley Cup. At age seventeen he was the center for the Montreal Lacrosse Team and the star halfback of the Britannia Football Team. He also won the Middleweight Amateur Boxing Title of Canada and was the Doubles Tennis Champion. From the age of seventeen through twenty-two there was no time during the year when his exploits did not appear in the press.

---

[2] According to my older brother's research, the "Little Men of Iron" did win the Stanley Cup in 1902, but William Cecil Christmas was not on the team. Our grandfather played primarily for the Montreal Amateur Athletic Association (M.A.A.A.) but may well have played for a number of other teams due to his yearlong participation in both team and individual sports.

4   *Leavings*

As a teenager my father sowed many a wild oat– not all having to do with the ladies. One time, for instance, he went to the Laurentians[3] on a fishing trip with one of his lustier friends. Though only in his late teens Montreal sportswriters had already dubbed him "Billie Christmas, Prince of Halfbacks." Young women readily agreed. With his handsome face, curly brown hair, and winning ways the young ladies went gaga over him. Some went so far as to throw roses at his feet when he came onto the playing field. Here was a young man a florist would appreciate.

Anyway, the fishing trip had gone well. Both young men had had a great time. But something was needed, something to top it off. Then it hit Billie. They had one more night. Why not spend it at an inn? They didn't have to be themselves. His friend could be his guardian, and he could be an inmate being transported to the mental institution at Verdun.[4]

Entering the inn, the two young men went straight to the desk. Billie's eyeballs were rolling and his head was twitching.

"What's wrong with your friend?" the clerk at the desk asked.

"Oh, he's harmless," Billie's friend said. "I'm escorting him to the asylum at Verdun. You can see why. But we need a place to stay for the night."

Billie continued to roll his eyes and twitch.

"Are you sure he's okay?" asked the clerk. "He looks mighty weird to me."

"He's fine. Believe me," his friend said. "I'm a professional. I know what I'm talking about."

"Well, okay," the clerk said. "But keep that loon locked in the room. I don't want any complaints from the other guests. This is a respectable establishment."

"I promise," his friend said. "You won't see or hear us till we leave in the morning. You have my word."

And he kept his word. Indeed, they were about the last ones to come down to breakfast the next morning. Or–to put it more accurately–Billie was about the last one to come down. As with many country inns back then, the breakfast area was a converted living room located directly below the rooms with the staircase to one side.

---

[3]   Canadian hills located in Southern Quebec– north of the St. Lawrence River on the south edge of the Laurentian highlands.
[4]   City in Southern Quebec on Montreal Island.

Suddenly there was a tremendous commotion upstairs. Loud voices could be heard; beds and chairs hit the floor and shook the ceiling; a door was heard to slam. Then it happened: down the stairs sped Billie Christmas, "Prince of Halfbacks"– streaking in all his glory. And I mean STREAKING! For he was butt-naked! Running by the astonished clerk and bewildered patrons, Billie made straight for the door, his eyes ablaze and his arms gesticulating madly. He then scooted out the door, ran down the hill, and jumped into the lake.

Needless to say, it was not an extended stay. Both young men were immediately evicted.

6   *Leavings*

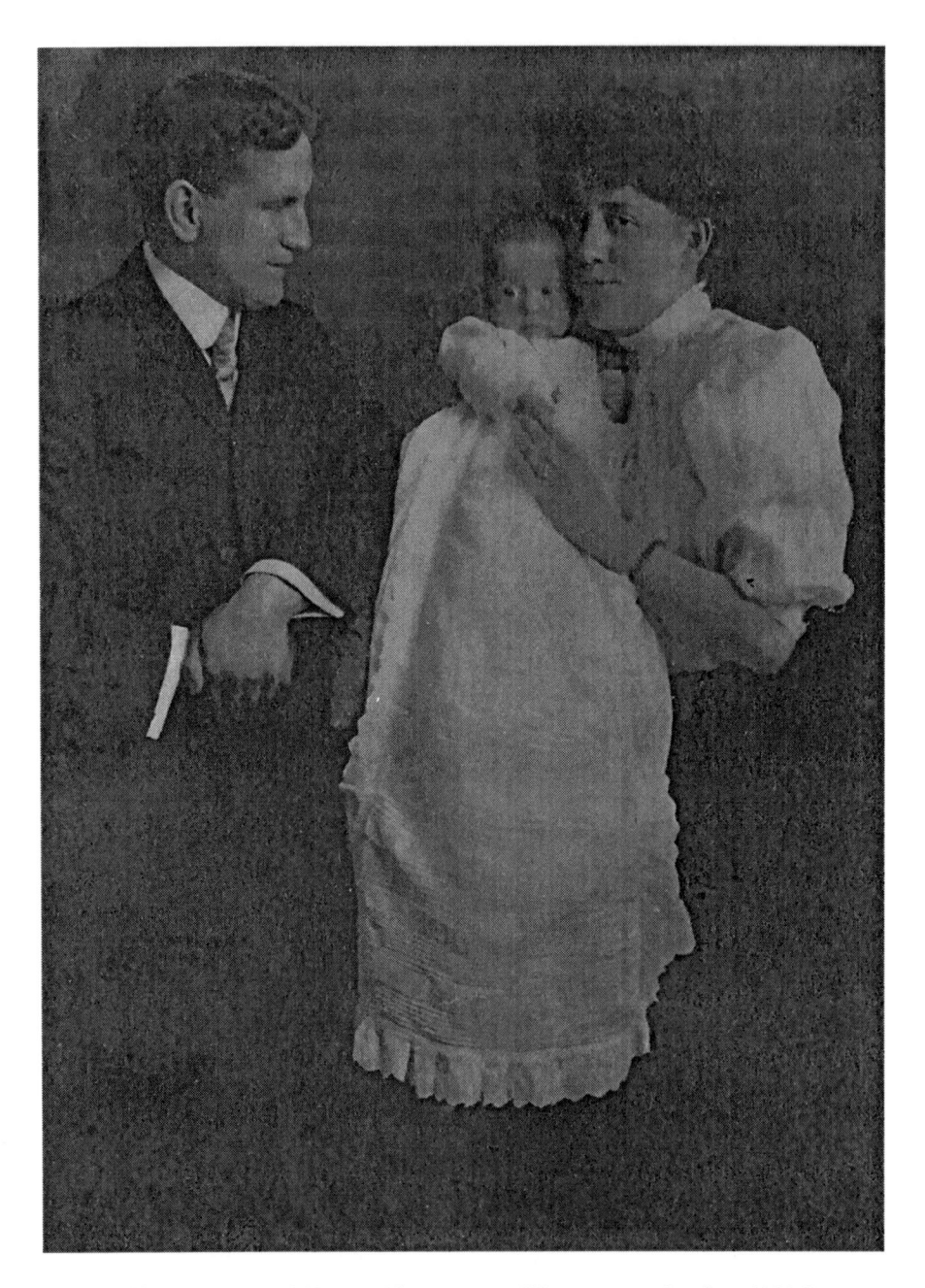

Billie, Doris, and Hattie Christmas in Westmount, Quebec (1906).
Christmas Family Collection

Chapter 2

EMBARRAS DE RICHESSES
Embarrassing Surplus of Riches

My father fell in love with my mother Ellen Harriet Turk when she was seventeen years of age and he was twenty-one. For him it was love at first sight. "Hattie" was a Toronto girl who was spending the summer in Montreal with her maternal grandparents whose home was near that of my grandfather. The Turks were native Montrealers and were wealthy in their own right. They were also Methodists and had married their daughter (my grandmother) to the young minister of their church– a common practice amongst well-to-do churchgoers in those days. At that time Methodist ministers were required to move every four years, which accounts for my grandmother being brought up mostly in Ontario. My grandfather was a dyed-in-the-wool fundamentalist. He was in no way an intellectual but could deliver a spellbinding sermon. Upon retirement, he became a come-to-Jesus evangelist. My mother and grandmother considered him to be a saint. My father and I sized him up as a lovable old fraud. The abiding love we had for my mother caused us to keep our assessment of his character strictly to ourselves.

My mother was a true saint. She was beloved by all who met her. The adjectives that best describe her are "gentle" and "good." My father often said, "Hattie, I respect your principles but don't for God's sake expect me to live up to them!" He nonetheless tried for I never heard him use a profane word in the house and, upon their engagement, became a "one woman man"– a marked departure from his premarital days.

My father was so enamored with my mother that he gave up athletics (at her insistence) at an age when most athletes are just entering their prime. He then moved to Toronto where he wooed and won her. Returning to Montreal after being married by his father-in-law at Owen Sound in June 1905, my father cashed in as a superstar athlete from a well-connected family by becoming a commissioned salesman. Money came his way easily so he soon struck out on his own as an importer of nuts and spices and other exotic foodstuff. The money–some twenty thousand dollars per annum–far exceeded anything he or my mother ever had and they spent it. They bought a fine house, complete with a cook, a maid, and a governess for my sister Doris (who was seventeen months my senior) and me. Doris and I were also enrolled in private schools as soon as we were old enough. During the summer my father rented a cottage on the lake for three months. He would then commute daily to and from the city. Such amenities were highly unusual in those days for a newlywed young couple, especially a couple without a vast inheritance of some kind. In retrospect, I don't believe my father considered the situation to be in any way abnormal. I can't recall business matters ever interfering to any extent with his home life. He felt that the amenities were merely his due for being a devoted husband and father.

My mother was a better than average pianist. She was a graduate of the Ontario Conservatory of Music, so we always had a piano in the house. Her playing was a continuous source of pleasure for the family. On the other hand, my father was not musically talented and neither was I. I was forced to take piano lessons for a few years before I was old enough to make my objections stick. I found playing the piano a nightmare. Somehow the message from my brain could not or would not connect with my fingers and the ivory. In fact, even playing the most elementary pieces was a soul-searing experience. Only my mother's determination and the avarice of my music teacher prevented the lessons from being terminated immediately. It was not a happy childhood memory.

The "good life" did eventually have some effect on my mother. For example, while partying she would sometimes take a glass of wine. Also, card playing and parlor games were permitted at home (never on Sunday)– both of which were anathema to Methodist minister's daughters in those days. In fact, my father had a passion for games both inside and outside the parlor. He always played to win. My mother would contrive to let him do so since it greatly added to his enjoyment and she couldn't care less. Mother certainly lacked the "killer instinct," so I inherited my attitude towards all sports from her. My parents were indeed an odd couple but theirs was an enduring love affair. They were most happy when at home with the family. This resulted in my having a happy childhood.

As expected, religion played an important role in our lives. Not a Sunday morning passed without the family going to church. We also went to church on Sunday evening when circumstances permitted. I attended Sunday school every Sunday afternoon from pre-school on. On the Sabbath the only books our parents allowed us to read were Foxe's *Book of Martyrs*, Bunyan's *Pilgrim Progress*, and the *Bible*. Foxe's book would have been better named *The Book of Horrors*. Nowadays it would be unsuitable for children's eyes. The *Bible* was considered so sacred that, under no circumstance, could another book be placed on top of it. On Sundays we were also not permitted to play outdoors, except in our fenced-in yards. Indeed, even parlor games were strictly forbidden. Though never particularly enamored with school, I found Sundays to be so depressing that I could hardly wait for Monday. My father must have shared my views for certainly Sundays were not so observed in his premarital days. Still, his love for my mother was such that he bore it all willingly.

10   *Leavings*

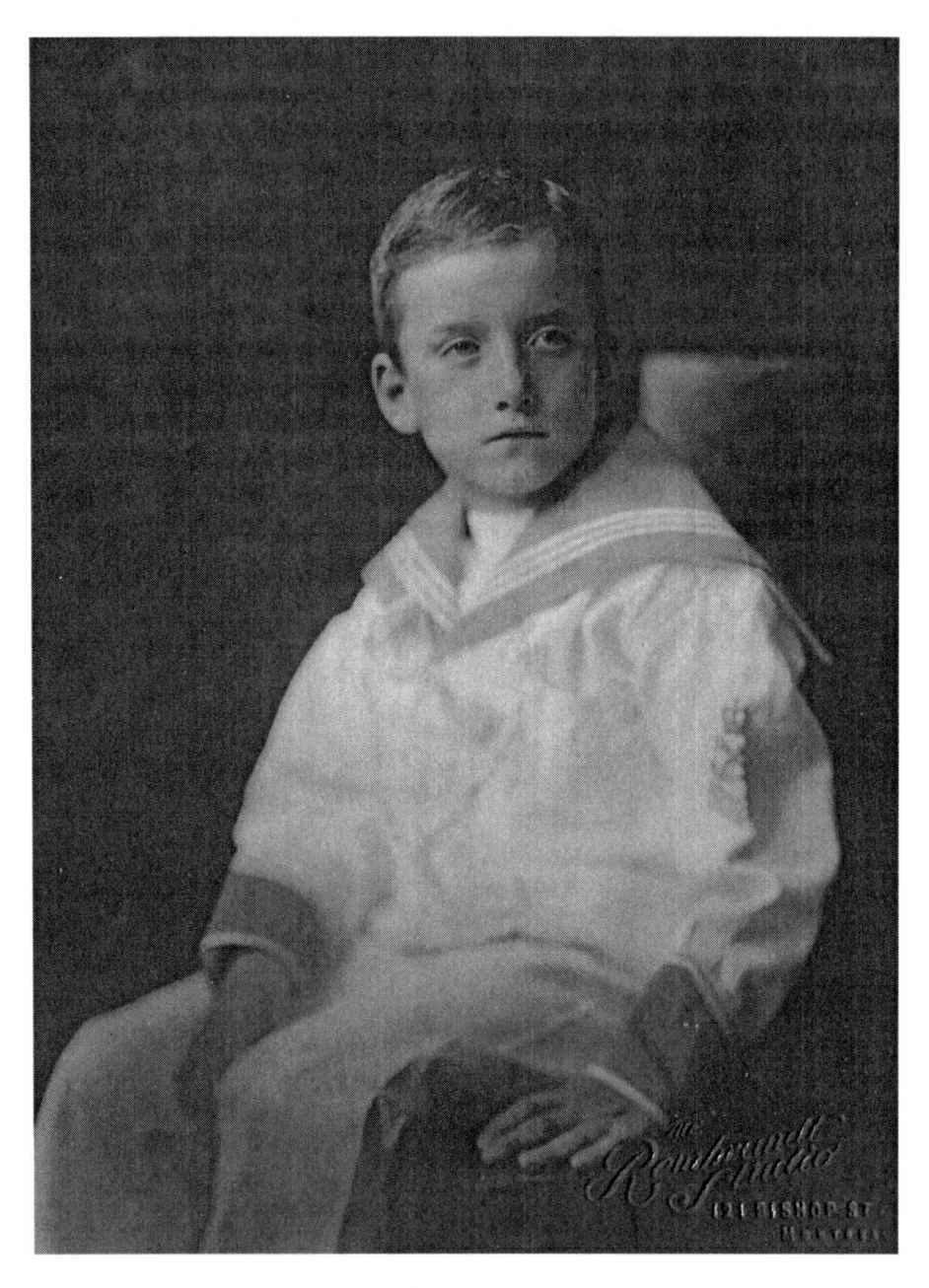

Dick Christmas as a young boy.
The choice of a sailor suit would prove to be prophetic.

Christmas Family Collection

Chapter 3

SANS SOUCI

Without Worry

Self-analysis is always difficult, but I would like to take a crack at it anyway. I was a precocious child but was not aware of it. This I attribute to ours not being an intellectual household. Indeed, my parents never pushed me though I do recall at a young age being paraded before guests to demonstrate my ability at spelling and mental arithmetic. Nothing was really made of it. My mother, however, spotting my preoccupation with books, always made sure plenty were within easy reach. To me what was in books was inconsequential. I would read anything. Then at a very young age I was very good at games, which suited my father. I recall a retired Englishman in the neighborhood who would let me visit his parrot Blixie if I would play chess with him. This was when I was too young to attend school. My precociousness was not a result of an extraordinary brain as much as a love for books at a very early age.

Of course, having a bright sister less than a year and a half my senior helped even though we fought like cat and dog. I was physically stronger than Doris, which she resented. We really loved, respected, and were proud of each other underneath it all. I must say more about Doris. Just before my parents' wedding my father asked his father what he should do about having children. It was a case of the blind leading the blind. My grandfather had eight kids at two-year intervals, and my father had been an athlete who in those days viewed a condom as being analogous to going to a circus with a paper bag over one's head. My grandfather said, "You and Hattie are both young and healthy so don't bother your heads about such matters." The result? Doris was born nine months and twenty days after the wedding, and I followed sixteen months later. After that my mother and father clearly made some adjustments in their sex life: my younger sister Louise didn't arrive on the scene until four years later.

In many respects Doris and I were much like twins. We even shared the same bedroom until we were of school age. We also celebrated yearly holidays, such as Christmas, with our parents since my father had become very much the family man.

Doris and I attended the same private kindergarten. Two sisters ran the school, and there were about twenty pupils. I was the only boy but unfortunately was too young to take advantage of the situation. The sisters introduced me to the *Elsie Books* and the books by Louisa M. Alcott.

The memory of my next school is only a blur, but the time I spent there was indeed a happy one. We played cricket and soccer when the weather was balmy and skated or played hockey when it was foul. My reading habits were temporarily derailed, but I paid no mind. By and large it was a rewarding experience mostly because I did not regard myself as mentally special.

The following year I was sent to a private school for boys, which was patterned on the so-called "public" schools in England. We called the principal "boss" behind his back, and the teachers called us by our surnames and referred to us as "men." I stayed there until I was ten years old when I had to withdraw due to my father's dire financial straits. Still, this school had a most salutary effect on me, namely it removed any sense I was extraordinary in any way. There were two categories of pupils: the boarders and the dayboys. I was one of the dayboys. Since the two groups were equally divided, I quickly became a well-adjusted creature of my environment.

Every minute of the day was carefully planned, and all activities required full and active participation of the entire class. Little or no time was spent being an individual. If one has never attended an English "public" school, I don't think one can fully understand the full import of such adages as "play up, play up, and play the game" and "it's not whether you win or lose it's how you play the game." There is a poem that states the Battle of Waterloo was won on the playing fields of Eton.[5] There is much truth to that. I do not believe that the British Empire would have been practicable if it weren't for the boys

---

[5] Actually "The Battle of Waterloo was won on the playing fields of Eton" did not come from a poem but first appeared as a quote in Fraser's *Words on Wellington* (1889).

with the "old school tie." It is said that Winston Churchill in seeking an aide was asked about what credentials were important. He replied, "Just send me a Harrow graduate"– Harrow being the public school he had personally attended. Whether the aide had attended Oxford or Cambridge University was inconsequential.

14   *Leavings*

Doris Christmas as a young girl. Doris was to live only five or six years after this picture was taken. She was just sixteen days shy of her sixteenth birthday at the time of her demise on March 4, 1922

Christmas Family Collection

Chapter 4

DE MAL EN PIS

From Bad to Worse

Doris was both beautiful and smart though not precocious like me. Physically she matured early and was soon attracting the attention of young men in their late teens and early twenties. One time, for instance, while riding on a train a middle-age man approached my father and said, "I would like to compliment your daughter, sir. I have never seen a woman's hair to equal hers."

The private schools Doris and I attended segregated the boys from the girls into separate classrooms. Doris and my interests therefore gradually diverged until we had an entirely different set of friends and quite different aspirations even though the family continued to be closely knit. Still, on several occasions I noticed something odd: an upperclassman would treat me with deference not out of respect but because of my gorgeous sister.

My father's luck ran out with the outbreak of World War I in 1914. I don't know all the details. It had something to do with his goods being confiscated by the Central Powers, and the insurance on said goods not being covered under the acts of war. My father wanted to declare bankruptcy and begin anew. His father, however, talked him out of it. "No man in our family has ever declared bankruptcy," he boomed. My grandfather then assured my father that he would stand behind him and would cover all losses. It was a hellish arrangement, and my father soon learned that it kept him in perpetual debt. As soon as he earned any money in a new venture, it immediately went to a creditor. It took some ten years before my father again became a free man. And it didn't end there, as you will see.

Somehow, my parents were able to keep our desperate straits hidden from us children. The disaster, however, was by no means strictly financial. For a time my father became a heavy drinker, but he would never drink around the house. Indeed, he soon gave up the sauce entirely, and the only evidence that he had ever had a drinking problem was the complete absence of alcohol in the house. That, I presume, was my mother's idea.

The trappings of affluence disappeared by degrees, never to return. The first to go were "the help." My mother took over all the housework, except for a washerwoman who came in once a week. Even our food changed drastically. No more fancy stuff. But my mother was proud. She had been a Palmer and a Turk and now she was a Christmas. She therefore refused to sell the house and bravely kept up appearances. I was too young to know what was going on but liked to fish. One day I went out and caught a mess of trout and brought them home for my mother to cook. Years later she said to me, "Remember those trout you caught that day? That was Heaven sent. We did not have enough to eat that night. It was that close." There were tears in her eyes.

Doris and I were not removed from private schools until three years had passed. We ceased going to the country in the summer, and my parents' weekly partying stopped. In fact, their social life came to an abrupt standstill. That did not seem to bother them, as my father had become a real homebody. We played all kinds of games together in the evenings for my father never seemed to tire of them. Finally there was the radio to listen to.

Despite our financial hardships my mother and father had a great life together until Doris became sick with that God-awful brain tumor. You don't know what a ghastly pall fell over the house at that time. First came the headaches; next the eyes crossed and her hair fell out; then came the pain and the morphine. The family doctor–a wonderful man–was at wits' end, not just for Doris but the whole family. Finally near the end he went into the bedroom alone. He was only in there a few minutes. Coming back out into the parlor, he said simply: "It's all over. She's gone." To this day I believe it was euthanasia. Bless him!

I mourned for the loss of my sister, but my grief did not compare with that of my parents. To this day I miss Doris, especially around Christmas. I have long since had no one with whom to share those happy days of our childhood.

Chapter 5

AU PAYS DES AVEUGLES LE BORGNE EST ROI

In the Land of the Blind the One-eyed Man Is King

After Doris's death something died in my mother. When a good woman loses a bright and beautiful daughter, she never recovers. She only learns to cope. Mother's way of coping was to turn to Christian Science. My father didn't like it, but there was nothing he could say or do.

The following year I was removed from private school and sent to a public school for non-Catholics in Westmount.[6] All non-Catholic schools in Quebec came under the jurisdiction of the Protestant School Board, whereas the parochial schools handled the Catholic students. In those days the boys and the girls were in separate classrooms. In fact, in my school the classrooms for the boy and girls were located at different ends of the building. The only time the two sexes were together was at recess, which resulted in no commingling whatsoever, except for an occasional pairing off of pupils who "matured young." Believe me, I did not fall into that category.

High school bored me. My reading had taken me far beyond what was covered in the textbooks, and mathematics came to me naturally. Lazy by nature, I was never considered a "grind." Apparently I had inherited from my father the ability to get along with all sorts of people. I was equally at home with both the jocks and the grinds and all the kids betwixt those two extremes. I was never a leader, however. I cannot recall being elected to any class office, be it president, vice-president, treasurer, or even secretary. In the tenth grade boredom coupled with the dire financial situation at home got the better of me, and I decided to drop out of school. My parents would have none of it. In protest I adopted a form of passive resistance, and for a year and a

---

[6] A Montreal suburb.

half sat with the slugs of the class in the back of the room. Seeing that my parents were not about to relent, I eventually gave up and resumed my former status. Still, the time I had spent with the amiable dunderheads was not wasted. We talked nonsense, cracked jokes, and had great fun together. Without girls in the classroom we could say whatever we wanted and often did. It was grand.

In the summer of 1923 at the age of seventeen I fell in love for the first time. Though the girl was in my class at Westmount High School, I had not met her there but in Val-Morin[7] where both our parents owned lakeside cottages.

The romance was a bittersweet experience for me. While having two sisters, I never thought of them as girls. Due to my extensive reading, I placed the poor girl on a pedestal and never once ever attempted to kiss her. She was popular, pretty, and nice, and our parents certainly approved of our dating. The affair carried over into the fall. I continued to take her out once every week as that was all I could afford, for most high school kids did not work in those days. I still remember her with great fondness though she gave me the air the next summer for another boy in Val Morin whose parents let him use the family car for dates on the weekends. Some things never change.

Nonetheless, this young lady had a great influence on my life. By giving me the air, she had not only blighted my summer vacation but hurt me as well. As a result, at the outset of the 12th grade I decided to show all and sundry what I could do if I really applied myself.

The result was spectacular and changed the course of my life. In the prestigious Provincial School Leaving Examinations (doesn't that have a better ring to it than End-of-Grade Tests!) I would have placed first in the advanced algebra and plane geometry exam had I not been so cocky and failed to see three questions on the back of the test. Racing through the seven questions on the front side, I brazenly handed in my test a good thirty minutes ahead of time.

"Young man," the tester whispered, "why didn't you answer the last three questions?"

I was stunned.

"What last three questions?"

"The ones here," he said pointing to the flip side of the page.

"Oh, I didn't see those. Please give me my test back. I can answer them in a flash."

---

[7] A municipality located in the Laurentian Highlands.

"Sorry, I can't do that. Once you give me your test, I can't return it to you. The rules are the rules."

As a result, I received a 70 instead of a 90 or a 100. Even with that poor showing, however, I still came in second and was awarded a scholarship to attend McGill.[8] Who beat me? Why the guy I had tutored, of course.

---

[8] Situated in downtown Montreal, this famous university is often referred to as "the Harvard of Canada."

Chapter 6

MAUVAISE HOUTE

Bashfulness

My father was in many ways more than a parent to me. He was, in fact, my best friend. I found him to be natively very intelligent though uninformed in subjects of depth and substance. We were formidable partners both at bridge and in golf. In most instances others playing with us insisted that the partnership be broken up. The contrast between my father's disinterest for intellectual matters and my fascination for them never detracted from the love and affection we had for each other. I respected his tastes as he respected mine. My having a reasonable natural ability for athletics helped considerably even though I sadly lacked the competitive spirit.

I fear that my non-competitive nature may have been transferred to the both of you. In my case it was exacerbated by my mother's not wanting to beat anybody at anything. A competitor she was not! On the other hand, my father had become ambivalent toward athletics due to the effect they had had on his life. Going from an adolescent superstar to total withdrawal from team sports as a young man, he knew the transitory nature of public adulation. Being a good father, he took me to see many games when I was a kid. I can distinctly recall being in the stands with the fans all around him on their feet screaming hysterically while he remained stoically seated, not bothering to rise to see what the commotion was about. He remained competitive by nature, but the I'd-die-for-dear-old-Rutgers syndrome was not part of his being. And that attitude rubbed off. I clearly remember watching the Boston Celtics play the St. Louis Hawks at the Boston Garden in the 7th and deciding game on their way to their first NBA championship. The game was decided in double overtime with my son

"Little Jud"[9] screaming "This is too close!" I finally got to my feet not because I was greatly moved but merely because the fans in front remained on their feet. I wondered at the time why they had bothered to buy seats rather than stay in the cheaper standing-room-only section.

Having a great athlete as a father and personally observing the influence fame on his life have led me to the conclusion that honoring athletic achievement in the White House is totally idiotic and an indictment of present-day American life. Indeed, the same can be said for anyone from the entertainment world. Great athletes, at best, possess a fleeting commodity in the fickle eye of the public. Dressed in garb that makes them look like creatures from outer space, they almost invariably have nothing to offer of permanent worth, and the wealth that is showered on them by an adoring public more often than not ruins them for life. As time passes and their particular talent wanes, they are often left defenseless to face the hardships of life. If this be our gods, heaven help us. As for autographs, what in heaven's name do people do with them?

With girls I was a hopeless romantic. I can probably attribute that to having read so many historical romance novels as a kid. No one had to tell me about the birds and the bees, for I was more aware of the biological roles men and women play than my parents. The Victorian Age viewed the sex act as repulsive, something nice women only submitted to as a duty to their husbands. All other women were loose and gave one venereal diseases. That girls might also have sex fantasies never entered my mind. Females had to suffer childbirth due to the curse laid upon Eve in the Garden of Eden. It was as simple as that. I therefore sympathized with the plight of all women, except my mother and two sisters who, for some irrational reason, did not seem to be part of the equation. As a result, I was both attracted and repelled by girls– attracted since I did not have homosexual tendencies and repelled because I did not wish to be the instrument of the Devil's or of God's wrath– whichever came first. Talk about a nut!

My peculiar attitude toward the fairer sex persisted throughout college and for a few years into my business career. I never kissed woman or even held hands until marriage. I had two fairly serious crushes, which is hard to understand since I must have seemed like a Jesuit priest on a date. In fact, I was silly enough to be flattered when a

---

[9] William's younger son Girard Richard Christmas

girl's mother said, "You two can stay out as late as you want. I need not worry since you are with Dick." If that was not the "kiss of death," I don't know what was. Still, I felt flattered. I cannot understand why any girl in her right senses would give me the time of day. I was ridiculous.

    Clearly I was an extreme case but far from the exception given the times. Mine was a middle class community and, as such, the families were riddled with Victorian concepts. Adolescent boys were thought to have beastly instincts, which any decent adolescent girl found disgusting and would only yield to after marriage. Though high school romances would on occasion ripen into marriage, they were still relatively rare and caused considerable concern amongst parents of the children concerned. Usually the attractive 11th and 12th grade girls were the ones that deviated from the norm. Much to the dismay of the high school boys, these girls dated and mated with older, more affluent suitors. Actually the system was not a bad one. Ironically it was the females, not the males, who insisted that they be removed from their pedestals at the end of World War I. This triggered a social revolution whose sexual ramifications we feel to this day.[10]

---

[10] Circa 1985

Chapter 7

A BON CHAT, BON RAT

To a Good Cat, a Good Rat

While the Christmases were a well-to-do middle class family, none of the eight brothers had gone to college. All had finished high school, but my going to college did not sit well with them. What was I trying to prove– that I was better than they were? Even my father was not terribly thrilled about my academic achievements. Though not against my going to McGill, he could not see how it could better me as a man. By nature very bright, my father never thought of using his natural endowments in his formative years other than to excel at competitive sports. I guess one could call it his intellectual blind spot.

That may sound odd to you, but it was not unusual in those days. The average middle class male back then was expected to glance at the newspaper headlines, read the sports page, and to go to church on Sundays– that being the sum total of his intellectual endeavors. Now don't disparage that attitude too quickly. On the whole, there was far less crime back then than nowadays, and there were certainly far less unnatural practices, sexual and otherwise. Moreover, as individuals and as a class, the men and women in those days willingly accepted as gospel any propaganda that the powers-that-be dreamt up. For the most part this enhanced domestic tranquility, except occasionally amongst the lower class– dubbed the "dangerous class" in Victorian England.

I entered McGill in the fall of 1925. I chose engineering as a major simply because most of my friends had done so. I hadn't the foggiest notion what I wanted to do with my life. Over the years I had acquired excellent study habits, and these now stood me in good stead, except at the drawing board where I struggled with descriptive geometry and blueprints. Nonetheless, by the end of my sophomore year I was first in three subjects: mathematics, physics, and mechanics.

One day a professor from the mathematics department pulled me aside.

"Dick," he said, "In my humble opinion you should switch your major from engineering to mathematics. You would be much happier with us."

"I would love to," I said. "But that would mean staying an extra year at McGill just to fulfill your prerequisites."

The oddest look crossed the professor's face followed by a wry smile.

"Listen, Dick," he said. "There are rules for regular students then there are rules for students like you. Do you understand?"

"Oh," I said stupidly.

And that is how I became a math major.

My grandfather Thomas Henry Christmas died in 1927. At that time my father had managed to bring the family finances up to the middle class level. At his death Thomas Henry or "Little Harry" left eight sons who were his residual legatees since my grandmother Jennie had died several years earlier. My grandfather left an estate in excess of one million dollars. Each of his sons therefore stood to receive two-hundred thousand dollars plus, which in those days was a tidy sum of money.

In going through my grandfather's effects, however, the executors uncovered a number of ancient checks that had been made payable to my father's creditors. As previously noted, my father had wanted to declare bankruptcy at the time, but his father, to save face, had made a gentleman's agreement whereby the debts would be paid off without my father owing a dime. In other words the money had been a gift, not a loan. There was no evidence anywhere in my grandfather's papers, however, to indicate that that was the case. Still, my grandfather had told three of his sons about the arrangement (one of whom had recently died), and the two surviving sons bore witness that their father frequently remarked how proud he was of the way my father had weathered the storm. Nevertheless, when it came to a vote, the other four sons voted to charge these checks against the share of my father's estate. This effectively disinherited him.

I heard this story not only from my father's lips but also from the lips of the unmarried son who had been closest to him. This uncle expressed great shame at the greed of his four brothers. Two of these brothers even removed the furniture from their father's house and sold it before the funeral, thus forcing the other brothers to rent furniture for the viewing of the body. At the time these two episodes did not seem to be of singular importance, but all that changed two years later when the Great Depression hit and my mother died a slow, agonizing, and expensive death from cancer of the breast. My father never really recovered from those twin blows.

During my freshman and sophomore years I had no need to join a fraternity since most of my classmates were friends dating back to high school. By my junior year, however, many of my friends had joined fraternities, and I was beginning to feel more and more isolated. I therefore decided to become a member of Sigma Chi, a decision that I never regretted. Still, the social life for McGill students in those days was limited. Due to the Great Depression students lived at home just as they had in high school.

Somewhere between my junior and senior years at McGill I became a nondenominational Christian. In a word I believed Christ to be the most remarkable human being that ever lived. Given his humble birth and background, he must have been divinely inspired. Whether or not he was divine and performed miracles, I felt was inconsequential. More importantly whether or not he was the Son of God was totally irrelevant. What mattered to me was what he taught and how he lived. Indeed, he was more than a messenger from God. He was an evolutionary punctuation created to save mankind from excessive greed, hypocrisy, and corruption. Such a point of view is consistent with traditional monotheism since it places the Creator above his Creation and gives him the power to alter said Creation at will. The Muslims have a point when they say that God's messengers are part and parcel of a higher religious creed.

I graduated from McGill in the spring of 1929 with no idea what I wanted to do. In those days there was really no field of endeavor for a mathematician or even a physicist, except academic work. Along with a majority of the community I held math and science professors to be nothing more than wooly-headed theorists– men and women with even less credibility than PhDs in the arts. Being one of the boys, I never considered teaching math at the college level as a life's work. Not until years later would I realize my folly.

I first heard about actuaries at the Sun Life Assurance Company where I had worked for three summers. Despite the fact that actuaries were not academics, I still felt an antipathy towards mathematics. There were others, however, who thought otherwise. As a result, I had several attractive offers, the most prestigious being a scholarship to study the Theory of Numbers and Mathematical Logic with the redoubtable Bertrand Russell at Cambridge University. I was also told a position with a prominent stockbroker was mine for the asking. Completely confused, I took a temporary job at the Sun Life to think things over. With letters of recommendation from both my professors and the president of McGill, it was assumed I would be an actuarial clerk.

I had my second serious crush in the summer of 1929. It was a weird coincidence. As with my father she too was a Toronto girl. Instead of visiting her grandparents, however, this young lady was visiting her aunt and uncle. Unlike my father I did not move to Toronto to press my suit. I did make a couple of trips to Toronto to see her, but the 720-mile roundtrip was too much for my paltry pocketbook. I was flat broke in less than a month! The whole affair had to be abandoned when the New York Stock Market crashed in late October precipitating the Great Depression. Sadly I now had more practical matters to attend to.

The Great Depression wiped my father out for a second time. As related, he had battled back valiantly from the first setback, and the family had enjoyed comparative prosperity if not affluence, which miraculously coincided with my four years at McGill. During that time Dad had become what was called "a manufacturer's representative." In other words he had a monopoly to sell the products of a particular manufacturer. Unfortunately these products were luxury items, hence money became scarcer and scarcer as the market dried up. Thereafter he earned barely enough to sustain himself and his family.

As for me, I went from having all sorts of goodies to being grateful to being an underpaid actuarial clerk. Most of my friends from college had graduated in engineering and at least half of them could not find work. Those students from affluent families who could qualify returned to college for postgraduate studies, but the rest by and large became disheartened bums. Some were even ruined for life. For the life of me I could not understand how Canada with its overabundance of natural resources would tolerate starvation and enforce idleness of its best and its brightest young people. This led to an intense, private study of economics– a move that drastically altered me intellectually. While I continued to do office work to earn a living, any thoughts about taking the actuarial exams went out the window. Instead, I read book after book on economics way into the wee hours and did not hesitate discussing my findings with others. That was stupid for the

Sun Life was a bulwark of the established order. During good economic times the company would tolerate superficial criticism, but with the Great Depression corporate executives circled the wagons and cut off all dissent. One could make a pass at the chief executive officer's wife at an office party, and it would be brushed off as the exuberance of youth. If, however, a person criticized the capitalistic system in any way, he was branded a Pink-o at best and a Red at worst for the remainder of his life. And I do not exaggerate here. McGill, being a private institution, was heavily endowed. Two promising young lecturers from the economics department publicly expressed a favorable opinion on some aspects of democratic socialism. Both men were hostile to what had transpired in Russia. That, however, did not stop prominent businessmen from moving against them. Pressure was soon brought to bear against the university itself, and the two men were fired.

I never was so honored although any future I may have had with the company had been irreparably damaged. I recall one of the company's executives calling me into his office. He had been speaking with the Head of the Mathematics Department at McGill who asked, "How is Christmas doing?" On being told that I was not writing the actuarial exams, the Head said, "He should be given a quick kick in the ass."

It was not, however, entirely my fault. I belonged in academic work. Had I known about economics before going to college, I would have majored in that subject or at least in history, for I had an excellent background in the latter. While I could have returned to do postgraduate work in mathematics or physics and done so on scholarships, to pursue an academic career in either economics or history would have required that I spend three more years as an undergraduate and another three more years as a graduate student before I could obtain a doctorate with no scholarships in sight. Being inherently lazy, I just could not face paying that price, especially when consideration was given to the dire economic straits of my family.

Actually I could have become a working member of the Canadian Communist Party. But there too I found myself to be very much the maverick. I attribute that to my extensive grounding in history. In Russia, where communism was supposed to lead to social democracy, an entrenched ruling class had formed under Stalin. This new ruling class would not, under any circumstances, give up the perquisites and privileges they enjoyed in order to establish a "dictatorship of the proletariat." While modern capitalism had its faults, I could not feature it being abandoned for communism since that would be an end to our political system and our liberties. I found myself slap dab in the middle, which rendered me impotent when the issues became sharp. As long as opposing factions hold to the barbaric adage "Either you are for me or against me," human beings will fail to become civilized.

Being in a twilight zone betwixt capitalism and communism limited my sphere of action. In my humble way I did what I could. For instance, I organized a group in the office into what we called "The League for Intellectual Advancement,"[11] which flourished as long as I was its inspirational leader. Over time, however, what had begun as an insatiable thirst for knowledge about economics gave way to distrust for any active involvement with the many movements that preached solving all of humanity's problems. Unknowingly I had highly schooled myself to be immune from all crackpot economic doctrines extant. This did not come without a price. Never again would I be indifferent to current affairs or to the developments influencing them. As a result, I began studying other subjects such as anthropology, biology, radio astronomy, and so on. These interests made the pursuit of the highest offices in the business world downright unattainable. More importantly the blinkers had fallen from my eyes rendering me ripe for love.

---

[11] See Appendix II for its Constitution.

Major Leo Edmond Hudon during World War I (circa 1915). Upon his graduation from the Royal Military Academy (RMC), Leo joined the Royal 22nd Régiment ("the fighting Van Doos") whose subsequent exploits have made it the most celebrated francophone regiment in Canadian history.

Christmas Family Collection

Chapter 8

EN FAMILLE

With One's Family

The Hudon household was complicated, even by French Canadian standards.

Your grandmother Hudon has an interesting life history. Her maiden name was Christin and the family resided in Ottawa. The family was wealthy and cultured and had made its money on a successful line of soft drinks. Unfortunately the money was lost through gambling. Mrs. Hudon's mother[12] and father[13] seem to have gone their separate ways with the mother being left to care for the children. Being an accomplished opera singer, she could not take good care of her daughter, so she enrolled her in a convent school in Oakland, California. There your grandmother received a solid education but became positively biased toward English-speaking Canadians. This I have always found odd, for she would later not only marry a French Canadian but also remain equally at home with both languages.

Mrs. Hudon had been a strikingly handsome woman. I did not meet her until she was in her late forties. By then she was overweight but still possessed great vivacity and sociability. She and her oldest daughter Lucille were like sisters and, as such, acted as twin hostesses whenever they threw a party. And with the parties lasting late into the night a great time was had by all.

Mrs. Hudon had an ironclad constitution and along the way developed the habit of drinking a fifth of gin a day. She never got up before noon and only ate one full meal a day. This meal, however, was an excellent one, which she fixed herself. She had very few friends

---

[12] Emeline Lamolte
[13] Charles A. Christin

being satisfied to live vicariously through the social whirl of her five gorgeous daughters. Mrs. Hudon handled her liquor like a lady, and Lucille was the only girl who drank at all.

Your grandfather Hudon came from a family that was highly regarded in Montreal. He was a handsome man, fifteen years his wife's senior. When war was declared in 1914, they were living in Montreal with six children. Mr. Hudon had received his education at the Royal Military Academy (the Canadian equivalent of West Point) at a time when French Canadian graduates from the academy were nearly non-existent. Great pressure was therefore brought to bear for him to join the French-speaking regiment as a major even though he was nearly fifty years old. He finally agreed to accept the assignment after his younger brother Albert agreed to keep an eye on his brood. The regiment was trained forthwith and was sent overseas where your grandfather distinguished himself.

In many respects your grandfather was the tragic figure in the Hudon home. Having left for France with a bilingual wife and six French-speaking young children, he returned some four years later to find all but his oldest child to be completely Anglicized. To compound matters, his battle wounds and various ailments made him a semi-invalid till his death in 1927. Marcelle often told the family that her father was extremely lonely and spent much of his time alone in his bedroom reading and playing solitaire. So much for a hero's welcome home.

I cannot blame anyone for this. Mrs. Hudon did what she thought was best for her children. In those days Quebec was a different place than it is today. English-speaking Canadians openly discriminated against their French-speaking brethren in all walks of life. Any clearheaded Canadian could see that the French-Canadians with their larger families would someday find their place in the sun. But this was not evident to the general public back then. Marcelle's father's disabilities combined with his inability to adjust to his home life essentially made Mrs. Hudon the de facto head of the house. It was a crown she would never relinquish.

At war's end the Hudon family consisted of six children. Geraldine would soon follow and become the last of the seven children. Two were boys: Gerard and Alain. Gerard was the oldest child and a brilliant shortwave radioman having been a member of an Artic Expeditionary Force at the age of eighteen. Alain was a sad case. Being mildly retarded, he picked up both English and French simultaneously and, when speaking, would mix the languages together. Today, Alain would have received specialized training and been a productive member of society, for he had a sweet disposition and loved hard work. But back then such training was rare and reserved only for the upper classes of which Alain did not belong. His was a sad, lonely, and frustrated life.

That left Mrs. Hudon with four and later five daughters to rear. Lucille was a strikingly beautiful woman with the coloring and complexion reminiscent of Elizabeth Taylor in her prime. She never had to lift a finger to attract men. They hovered around her like bees around a honey pot. Four years behind Lucille came the twins, Madeleine and Marcelle. Pert, petite, and pretty with long brown hair and sky-blue eyes that evoked an odd mix of innocence and penetration, they exuded a femininity the likes of which I have never seen before or since. They were more than "double trouble." They were double trouble to the nth degree.

After the twins came Jeanne, the natural athlete of the family. More handsome than beautiful, Jeanne was born out of place, out of time. Had she been born today, she would have garnered any number of athletic scholarships. But in those days women athletes were frowned upon. Only women like Babe Didrikson[14] were able to carve out a niche, to find their way in the world.

Last came Geraldine, yet another beauty much along the lines of the twins but a tad taller. Geraldine would eventually mature into a stunner whose sense of humor eerily mirrored that of her mother's. I can never remember talking with her without her telling me a joke. And a damn good one at that!

Mrs. Hudon possessed many sterling qualities. First, she had a vibrant personality with an intelligence way above average. She was especially stimulated in the company of young, boisterous men. She enjoyed both hearing and telling bawdy jokes. She would not, however, permit jokes that were raunchy and unsuitable for the ears of a middle-class Victorian matron.

Mrs. Hudon also was a skilled musician and could play the piano by ear. Indeed, nothing pleased her more than banging away at the keys late into the wee hours surrounded by the voices of her sober

---

[14] Mildred Ella "Babe" Didrikson Zaharias (1911 - 1956) was the greatest female athlete of her day. Excelling in golf, basketball, and track and field, she evinced many of the talents of the legendary Jim Thorpe.

daughters and their not-so-sober beaux. She herself drank but handled her liquor well. Of course, she had hangovers but accepted them "like a man." Nevertheless, she demanded respect and got it. That set her apart. Somehow she knew how to win the respect of both young men and young women and still have a rollicking good time. No wonder her daughters adored her.

Marcelle was therefore brought up in a feminine household dominated by her mother, and she loved it. Passive by nature, she had read Louisa May Alcott's classic *Little Women*, which instantly became her most cherished novel. She relished women's talk, especially with her sisters, and got a bigger kick from their experiences than she did her own. She became their confidante and was appreciated as such. So much so that upon her death one of her sisters said to me: "Marcelle had a special quality, something that endeared her to everyone in the family. Don't ask me to describe what the special quality was. It was just that– *special*."

There were times, however, when that specialty worried Mrs. Hudon. She once told me with some concern that she and Marcelle had once gone to the movies, and Marcelle had slipped her hand into hers saying: "Now I am happy for I am with my mummy." Of course, Marcelle thought this was an entirely asexual act. Her mother, on the other hand, wasn't all that sure. Then on another occasion Mrs. Hudon said pointedly to me: "My other daughters can take care of themselves, but not Marcelle. I swear if a man ever hurts her I'll kill him." A warning that meant nothing to me, for to hurt Marcelle in any way was inconceivable.

Jeanne Alice (nee Christin) Hudon in full gaslight regalia (circa 1900). Jeanne met Leo at a family reunion in Ottawa. He was a 3rd cousin and sixteen years her senior

Christmas Family Collection

Chapter 9

ENFANT GATE
Spoiled Child

Into this pleasant setting slithered the serpent, Reggie Molson. Some nineteen years older than the twins, Reggie had fallen hard for Marcelle whose appearance in the Investment Department had caused quite a stir. Marcelle soon caught him staring surreptitiously at her as she went about her work. Nonetheless, he was cordial and friendly and did not make advances other than casual conversation. Eventually he did make his move and ran into stiff competition. Reggie, however, was used to that. He was a man with ample ammunition.

At the time Reggie was living in a posh apartment with his recently widowed mother and her sister. In Montreal the name Molson carries the same prestige as the name Vanderbilt does in New York. Reggie therefore enjoyed all the trappings that came with great wealth. He belonged to the "best" clubs and traveled extensively with his mother to such places as the Lake Placid Country Club to which he belonged. He also rented a country house with a friend and drove his own car in addition to being chauffeured in the family limousine. No one else in Marcelle's orbit could begin to match such affluence and purpled ease.

Surely Mrs. Hudon viewed Reggie as the "Catch of Catches." Furthermore, Reggie's mother thought Marcelle was a darling, the perfect mate for her son. But Marcelle wanted none of it. Instead of embracing Reggie as a suitor and possible husband, she found him "physically repulsive" and, worse yet, a threat– someone who could break up the lifestyle she loved and longed to preserve. Neither Reggie nor Mrs. Hudon really understood this. Both were terribly status conscious, whereas Marcelle – at least as a young woman – was not. She once said to me: "You know, Dick, after my spat with Reggie, I lost the respect of my family. It was like I had let them down, like I had committed a crime."

In a way she had.

Chapter 10

ANCIENNE NOBLESSE
Old-time Nobility

The history of the Molson family is a long and storied one. One John Molson came over to Canada from "the old country" many generations back. He was a man of great energy and drive. More importantly he had a genius for business. He started with a modest tavern on the waterfront but rapidly expanded into various enterprises, the two most notable being the Molson Bank and the Molson Brewery. Furthermore, John Molson's descendents not only inherited his gift for making money but also had the rare good sense not to spend it. In doing so, they were not a stingy bunch. They shared their wealth with the community by supporting a number of charities and funding worthy civic projects. In a word, they rightly deserved their good name.

Having died in the prime of life, Reggie's father was unable to leave his stamp on civic affairs. Still, at his death he was a wealthy man, and his wife had riches in her own right. With only one younger brother Reggie could be expected to inherit a fortune upon the death of his mother. He therefore decided to oversee the family fortune himself. This was a wise move. Reggie worked in the Investment Department of the Sun Life. Since this arm of the company invested heavily in common stock, Reggie knew where to invest and where not to invest the Molson money.

Reggie Molson never seems to have spent an evening at the Hudon home. His routine went like this. He picked up the twins after work and drove them home to their mother's apartment. At the apartment the twins would either stay at home or be taken out by Reggie for entertainment. If he took them out, he would never go into their dwelling after taking them home. Instead, he would drop them off at the doorstep. On Sundays he had to alter his routine by driving directly to the apartment to pick them up. This system enabled him to monopolize the twins' time making it virtually impossible for them to have a normal social life. In a word, their home life outside of a place to sleep ceased to exist.

Reggie's mother and aunt liked Madeleine but adored Marcelle. After much coaxing, Marcelle accepted Reggie's ring on one condition: that it not be construed that they were engaged. Marcelle was on the up-and-up here. Never for a moment did she contemplate marrying Reggie. Indeed, it was just the opposite: she seems to have delighted in exasperating him. Reggie would tell her that she was prettier without lipstick. She would then smear it on twice as thick. Reggie would say she did not need perfume, that she had a "natural odor" all her own. She would then splash it on.

Meanwhile, Madeleine's nose was more than out of joint. It was disconnected. Marcelle had seen her staring at her while she was at her vanity making herself up. "Never," she would say later, "had I seen such an expression of hatred in my dear sister's eyes. It didn't take a genius to see the cause, but what could I do?"

Marcelle had a point. Madeleine would usually first attract the men, but the men would then end up mooning over Marcelle. Reggie reversed that process in spades. No matter how hard she tried, Madeleine could not attract Reggie in a romantic sense. Reggie, like many men, was enamored by the chase: the more he pushed his suit with Marcelle the harder she pushed back.

In an attempt to capture Marcelle's heart, Reggie began to date the twins as a unit. This was an excellent ploy, for it eliminated the need for a chaperone. But once on a date Reggie neglected Madeleine and concentrated on Marcelle. For instance, he would always insist that Marcelle sit up front next to him with Madeleine in the backseat of the roadster. This galled Madeleine to no end. In the past she had always been the main attraction, but now the roles were reversed. Still, Madeleine accepted her lot. And why shouldn't she? The "goodies" were too much to pass up, and Mrs. Hudon had encouraged her to stay involved.

Then it happened: *Madeleine fell madly in love with Reggie.* In her eyes he could do no wrong. This was not the case with Marcelle. She and Reggie quarreled incessantly. And the more they quarreled the more captivated he became. Such is the perversity of humans.

Chapter 11

ALEA JUCTA EST

The Die Is Cast

The Sun Life was a great marketplace for a young man seeking a wife. About seventy-five percent of the employees were middle class girls merely putting in the time until they would find a husband and fulfill their destiny as wife and mother. Parents considered the company a fine place to park their daughters as any hanky-panky between the sexes brought immediate dismissal for both parties. Marriage brought a similar fate to any female employee. The Canadian courts at the time stubbornly refused to extend equal employment rights to women on the grounds that it was unenforceable and against public policy. As a result, the Sun Life was teeming with nubile young lovelies eager for male companionship.

The Hudon twins joined the Sun Life when they were seventeen years old. They had worked for a short time at a bank not long after their father died in 1927. They had only finished the 8th grade and were the only ones in the family not to have finished high school. That was a shame but understandable. Being high school dropouts plagued them personally though to an outsider it was not noticeable. They were the youngest employees in the Sun Life. I suspect their Uncle Albert was instrumental in getting their jobs though no one in the office ever questioned their diligence or competence. They brought sunshine to everyone who worked there.

I was not alone in thinking that "the twins" were something special. They were beautiful, pert, vivacious, and sexy– very sexy. They wore identical homemade dresses– clothes that were tasteful yet highlighted their exquisite figures. They also displayed creativity with their hairdos. One such hairstyle utilized a small intricate braid going from one temple to the other. That might not sound like much, but details such as this set them apart. "The twins" were identical, and you had to know them well to physically tell one from the other. Both were avid tennis players and played with great regularity on the Sun Life tennis courts.

One day a friend of mine approached me and said: "Listen, Dick. I know you prefer golf to tennis, but really you ought to go and see 'the twins' play. Boy, are they an eyeful."

"No thanks," I said. "Most of my spare time is occupied with economics and world affairs. Anyway, don't you think they are a bit out of my league?"

"I wouldn't say that," he said. "At the moment both are unattached. That makes them fair game."

"That's not what I hear. Anyway, I don't want to be just another guy salivating at the trough. No thanks. This time I'll pass."

Still, whenever I saw either Madeleine or Marcelle in the hallway, I was distracted, very distracted.

As the months passed, however, my interest in politics and economics began to wane. No matter how much I wished otherwise, the deep flaws within the human psyche made the social and economic solutions to man's problems impossible– at least in the foreseeable future. I still found the twins captivating, and that bothered me. I therefore set out to date one of them.

"Surely they must be superficial in worldly matters," I said to myself. "All I have to find out is how shallow and silly they are. Then their physical allure will disappear."

In the summer of 1927 I had worked in the Claims Department with Madeleine. I knew several men in that department and was close to two in particular. Seeking a formal introduction, I approached one man and then the other. Both men politely rebuffed me saying each had a proprietary claim to Madeleine. I was shocked. Clearly this was not going to be easy. As Madeleine and I had mutual friends at the office, I next telephoned her at home and asked for a date directly.

"I'm sorry, Dick. My mother would not approve of that at all. We don't know each other well enough."

I was immediately struck by the soft, rich cadence of Madeleine's voice– a trait Bill Shakespeare claims is an excellent thing in women.

"Well," I said, "how about a double date? I will set up the whole thing. The four of us can go out on the town for dinner and dancing. How does that strike you?"

"Fine," she said. "But I must be on good terms with the other couple. No strangers. Promise?"

"I promise," I said.

I next called a close personal friend with whom the twins played tennis and explained my predicament.

"If you do this for me," I said, "there's dinner and dancing on me at the Windsor Hotel."

It was an offer he couldn't refuse. The Great Depression was well underway, and no one but the rich spent money so frivolously. He called me back in a matter of minutes saying the date had been set. The die was cast.

My father, catching word of my interest in Madeleine, laughed and said: "This is marvelous news! I'm a good friend with the twin's father Leo Hudon and an even better friend of his brother Albert. Indeed, Albert and I played on the same football team together. We also went at it many a time– with him wrestling and me boxing. I always got the better of him since I would never agree to fight in a confined place. I really had to dance around him. Had Albert ever gotten his paws on me, he'd have broken me in half."

Of course, hearing this made me shake my head in disbelief. But how was I to know? The twins spoke perfect English, whereas their father and uncle had a pronounced French accent. One would have never guessed that they came from the same family.

46   *Leavings*

Madeleine Hudon at the time she dated the author (1932). Though Dick fell for her on their first date, Madeleine did not return the compliment.

Christmas Family Collection

Chapter 12

FEUX D'ARTIFICE

Fireworks

Madeleine charmed my socks off on our first date. She was a little lady in the strictest sense of the word. Besides being a lively conversationalist, she was an angel to dance with. She possessed that rare gift of never trying to lead, of making her partner feel like Fred Astaire. By the time we said goodnight I was smitten. Before parting, I suggested another date, and she agreed to meet in a couple of days. I was elated. It never crossed my mind that it was odd for her to have so much free time, that there were no other suitors on the scene. Like any other moonstruck lad I was too thrilled to think straight. On our date the only mention of boyfriends had to do with Marcelle.

"My sister is engaged to Reggie Molson," Madeleine had said demurely. "She is wearing his ring."

I counted myself lucky. I had chosen the right twin.

For the next six weeks Madeleine and I saw each other three or four times a week. Of course, I was living in a fool's paradise. My meager funds prevented us from doing anything spectacular. But as far as I was concerned, that did not diminish our dates in any way. By the time Reggie returned from his Caribbean junket in March, I was hooked. All Madeleine had to do was reel me in.

Madeleine, of course, had no intention of reeling me in. Suddenly from seeing her three and four times a weeks I was lucky if I could see her at all. She was still friendly and spontaneous with me, but now a date had to be "confirmed" with her reneging more often than not. This exasperated the bejesus out of me. Finally I demanded to know what was going on.

"I'm sorry to be so fickle," she said. "But I now find myself in a most difficult and delicate situation."

"Oh really," I said trying to be sympathetic. "Is there anything I can do?"

"Yes," she said. "Please be patient. Last week I went on a dance date at the Windsor Hotel with my sister and her fiancé. I don't know what exactly happened, but Reggie did or said something that infuriated my sister. She won't even tell me what it was. Anyway, right in front of all those people, Marcelle took off Reggie's ring and flung it at him."

"She did what?"

"She flung his ring right into his face. It caused an awful furor. But that's not all. The ring bounced and rolled onto the dance floor. Everyone had to stop dancing and get down on hands and knees and look for it. It was so embarrassing."

Actually I thought it was funny as all hell and showed just how much pluck Marcelle had. If only I had been there to witness it. But I held my tongue.

"So how do matters stand now?" I asked with false innocence dripping from my fangs.

"They are not on speaking terms. Or, more accurately, Marcelle has frozen Reggie out. She never wants to see or hear from him again."

"It's over then?"

"I hope not. Marcelle and Reggie are deeply in love with each other. I just need to hold the fort until Marcelle comes to her senses. And that should be soon. Then you and I can start dating again."

All this was true. Madeleine had not really lied. She had *only* failed to tell me she loved Reggie with all her heart, and that a most awkward and strange relationship existed between the twins and the entire Molson household. It took me a couple of months to sort things out, but sort them out I did. Then I realized that Marcelle had never loved Reggie. It had all been a charade, and she never wished to see him again even though she liked his mother and aunt. For his part Reggie was able to resume his old lifestyle, only now he had only one twin at his beck and call. This arrangement, though not as perfect as the first, still satisfied Reggie's mother and aunt. Madeleine brought youth and beauty into their lives, something that had become a scarce commodity in the Molson household.

50   Leavings

Marcelle Antoinette Hudon as a young woman working for the Sun Life Assurance Company of Montreal (circa 1932). This picture was taken near the time Marcelle rebuked the author with the chilling "I will have none of my sister's leavings."

Christmas Family Collection

Chapter 13

J'ACCUSE

I Accuse

Marcelle's break with Reggie placed Mrs. Hudon in a serious dilemma. Anxious for one of her daughters to marry a Molson, she had to let go or fight to maintain the close family ties that had taken her years to establish. By nature a gambler, she chose to let go betting that Madeleine or Marcelle would marry Reggie and reunite with the family someday. She still possessed a trump card: not one but two of her daughters were deeply involved in Reggie's life. In the long run Reggie could not marry both but would have to choose between the two or vacate the scene. Mrs. Hudon did not see him vacating the scene. What she failed to foresee was Marcelle dumping him. To Mrs. Hudon that was a reckless and foolish act, an act for which Marcelle was never completely forgiven. Years later she would say to me, "As soon as I ditched Reggie, Mother preferred Madeleine over me. It had never been that way before. I had been so close to my mummy, much closer than Madeleine. But after the breakup all that changed, and Madeleine became mother's darling."

Once Marcelle's mind was made up, however, her mind stayed made up. At heart shy and retiring she lacked the "come hither look" that Madeleine had refined to a fine art. As a result, Marcelle now found herself adrift, with no boyfriends of any kind. To anyone who did not know her intimately this would have been an absurdity, for she was incredibly beautiful, provokingly sexy, and feminine to the core. Yet this was the predicament she found herself in. Luckily she was bright and still had her family to fall back on.

My relationship with Madeleine did not come to a head for months. But when it did I was perfectly blunt.

"Let's cut out all the foolishness," I said. "Let's act like the civilized people we are and face the truth: It is you, not Marcelle, who loves Reggie."

Her face went scarlet.

"No, that is not so," she said indignantly.

"I believe it is so," I said firmly. "And it has been so for many, many moons. There is no reason to be ashamed of it. Love is a wonderful thing, especially when it is reciprocated."

I overstepped my bounds here. I had no smoking gun and Madeleine knew it.

"Now see here, Dick Christmas. There is nothing between Reggie Molson and me. And you had better not spread such a rumor. I would never forgive you for that."

Within weeks a timely event occurred that enabled me to extricate myself. Gerard Hudon owned a 4-door De Soto sedan of recent vintage. He had lost his job and was hard up for cash so he suggested I rent the car for three months. That would serve two purposes: it would tide Gerard over till the fall and provide me with transportation to and from Val-Morin where I often played eighteen holes of golf with my father and two friends. I decided to take Gerard up on his proposition. I soon found that the car not only enabled me to get in much more golf but also had the ancillary benefit to pick up and drive the twins to work.

That broke the ice with Marcelle. Till then she had held me at arms length and for good reason. I had shown no interest in her during my mad pursuit of Madeleine. Now, seeing the situation clearly, my interest in Madeleine waned and waned fast.

Marcelle did not encourage my suit. Nonetheless, I can pinpoint the exact moment when my heart flipped from Madeleine to Marcelle. I had been driving the twins to work for a few weeks when one morning Marcelle bounded into the car clearly upset.

"Madeleine will be joining us in a few minutes," she said in a level but disturbed tone. "Please be careful what you say to her. She is not her genial self today."

Madeleine did come out in a few minutes crying her heart out. None of us spoke all the way to the office, and once there Marcelle and I discreetly got out of the car and entered the building leaving Madeleine alone to compose herself.

Naturally I was curious to know what Madeleine had found so distressful. By chance I met Marcelle that evening and asked her what it was all about.

"It's Reggie Molson," she said with an edge in her voice. "He telephoned Madeleine this morning and bawled her out for the dress she'd worn to the hockey game with him last night. He said it was too revealing. I don't understand my sister sometimes. Why on earth does Madeleine take such guff? I sure as heck wouldn't– Molson or no Molson!"

A light suddenly went on in my head. A few months earlier the twins had ceased wearing matching dresses. I had presumed that Madeleine, being the dominant twin, had initiated this change in attire. Now I knew otherwise. Madeleine's new attitude stemmed from Reggie's desire for the twins to look older than they really were. That way the disparity between Reggie's and Madeleine's ages would not be as pronounced. Predictably, Marcelle refused point blank to acquiesce to Reggie's request. Madeleine, on the other hand, hastened to do so to such a degree that Mrs. Hudon was appalled. Once Marcelle had withdrawn from the scene, Madeleine's clothes quickly resembled those of a middle-aged woman. She even ceased to use cosmetics of any kind. I was stunned with Madeleine's metamorphosis, with the way she kowtowed to Reggie's every whim. Sure, my heart went out to her but with such pity went much of my respect and all of my love for her. Suddenly I realized that Marcelle was made of deeper, sterner, and tougher stuff. And, yes, I now understood what Madeleine had meant when she said, "The men start out with me but end up with Marcelle." They had to. She was much more complex and intriguing.

That episode opened my eyes. I suddenly saw how wimpy, lame, and hopeless my infatuation with Madeleine had been. She loved Reggie and only Reggie. I could only hope that Reggie would one day come to his senses and see the diamond at his feet. She was a good kid and deserved that much.

Marcelle was no fool. She had not only lived through the entire drama but had also played a leading role in "the play within the play." Furthermore, she knew my feelings for her had changed drastically. This confused her for she had done nothing to encourage me. Obviously Marcelle liked me as a friend and wanted our relationship to stay that way. Still, I took the plunge and pressed her for a date.

"No way," she said curtly. "As far as I'm concerned, you are still my sister's boyfriend."

"That's not true," I said emphatically. "You know she loves Reggie– that her sole mission in life is to be a Molson."

"I'm not so sure about that. Surely Madeleine will tire of him. All you have to do is be patient."

"Oh, come off it, Marcelle. Stop speaking from the south end of the bull and level with me. Will you go out with me or not?"

She was incensed. No man had ever spoken to her like that before, let alone "a friend."

"I will have none of my sister's leavings," she said eyes ablaze.

"Please, Marcelle, you know very well that to the outside world you appeared to be Reggie's girl, and Madeleine appeared to be footloose and fancy free. How was I to know that the opposite was true, that Reggie's ring meant nothing to you and Madeleine was keeping me as a spare tire at best?"

She looked at me in dead silence with those soft, sensitive, sky-blue eyes– true windows to the soul. I tried to fathom their meaning, to come up with some sort of message. I failed.

"You say you want me as a friend, not a boyfriend," I said in desperation. "What exactly do you mean by that?"

"I enjoy being with you," she said. "You are such a good companion. You are kind and always treat me like a lady and –"

"And?"

"And you teach me a lot. I especially like the way you talk about literature and history. How did you ever learn so much?"

The question caught me off guard and I blushed.

"Anyway, I want to continue to see you from time to time," she said, "but nothing serious. *No dates*. I don't want people to think I'm attached to you."

Such an arrangement I thought pure folly. Nonetheless, I went along with it. I had never met a woman quite like her, not even her twin sister. Somehow I just couldn't stand the thought of losing her forever.

"All right," I said. "You win."

"Thank you, Dick. That means so much to me."

Chapter 14

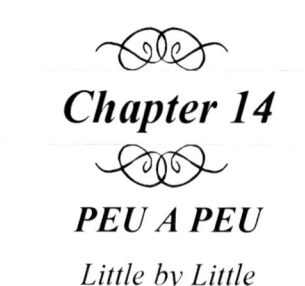

PEU A PEU
Little by Little

After turning the car back over to Gerard in September, Marcelle and I started taking weekly walks together. Often her baby sister Geraldine would join us. We chose walking rather than staying in the Hudon parlor since that allowed us to talk privately. Unlike Reggie I did not shun the Hudon household. Marcelle's family had a fabulous cast of characters. Indeed, it was impossible to dislike any of them. They were such genuine people. Still, I felt that Mrs. Hudon never quite approved of me. Being astute, she was aware of my unconventional ideas, especially my economic and political thought that bordered on the radical. This made me a dangerous suitor. I really could not disagree with her.

I continued to badger Marcelle for a date, but she kept me at arm's length like I was a leper from Molokai. With winter fast approaching, I knew our fall walks would soon end. So I pressed even harder for a date.

"I'm sorry, Dick," she said adamantly. "I'm fine the way things are."

By New Year's 1932 I had become the equivalent of a tabby cat in the Hudon home. The role sickened me. What was I waiting for? The day when the twins' charms had faded and one of them would turn to me in desperation for love and companionship? "No dice," I said to myself and promptly vacated the scene to dedicate my spare time exclusively to intellectual pursuits. I organized a small group of like-minded friends, and we began to meet regularly to discuss the social and political problems of the day.

My spasm with the twins had lasted a year and had left its marks. I often thought of them with fondness, especially Marcelle. On the rare occasions I saw them in the office my heart ached. I tried dating other women, but none gave me the deep sense of contentment the twins did. It would be a long, long time before I got them out of my system– if ever!

A year went by. Then one evening I received a surprise telephone call from Jeanne Hudon, Marcelle's younger sister.

"Hello, Dick. How would you like to come to our home this Friday? We're throwing a birthday party for the twins. They will be twenty-one on June 12th."

"I'd love to," I said. "When do you want me to be there?"

"Around six. Is that all right?"

"That's perfect. I'll see you then."

It was a delightful party. With Mrs. Hudon as hostess how could it be otherwise? There were only about a dozen guests. All were friends of Lucille and Gerard, except me. Why was that? Wasn't this supposed to be the twins' party? Then there was Madeleine. She was at the party but not of it. Clearly she had become totally absorbed with the Molson clan and was just putting in an appearance. I had Marcelle all to myself.

Our being separated for over a year never came up. As the party wound down, I screwed up my courage and made my move. After all what did I have to lose?

"Would you be interested in going out with me this weekend?" I asked.

"I'd love to," she said.

I was stunned. A year ago such a response would have been unimaginable. Now it seemed as normal and natural as breathing. We fleshed out the details, and I left the party elated.

I found Marcelle delightful. On our first date she chattered away prettily about her activities and was genuinely interested in subjects that fascinated me, especially history and poetry. Whereas Madeleine's sole topic of conversation concerned the Molson clan and what had transpired on her most recent date with Reggie, Marcelle liked to discuss any number of subjects and issues. The result was predictable: I fell head over heels in love with her.

I proceeded with caution. Initially we saw each other once a week. That, however, was soon doubled. I had planned to make that our routine, but then I bought my first car in August. That knocked everything into a cocked hat.

The car was a Ford Model A roadster. Its body had seen better days, but the engine was fine. I drove the darn thing all over the place, and it never let me down. During the several weeks prior to putting the car up on blocks for the winter, Marcelle and I cruised around town almost every night. Most of the time I would just drive and stop to have a hot dog or a hamburger before taking her home. I soon became her boyfriend though I never had the temerity to hold hands, let alone kiss her good night. We were just good pals.

In hindsight Marcelle and I had an odd relationship. I had few rivals despite her ample appeal to the opposite sex. That made dating her much easier, so I had little to complain about. Still, the situation was not without deep sexual overtones. Indeed, the more sensitive we were to one another's feelings the more suppressed our biological urges became. Nevertheless, I continued to move gingerly. I had learned from experience that Marcelle was easily spooked.

After putting the Model A up for the winter, Marcelle and I continued to date frequently, but it was not as much fun. Simply put, I lacked the funds needed to buy privacy and have her all to myself. The situation did, however, have a plus side. My extracurricular interests in economics and world affairs had effectively ruined my status as an actuarial student with the Sun Life. My feelings for Marcelle now made me reexamine my position with the company. The key question came down to this: how could I reinstate myself as a bona fide member of the actuarial program? The character of the company was peculiar. Despite the depression the company continued to grow at an unprecedented rate. In fact, management was now overstocked with actuarial students. These students fell into two groups: ten handpicked men from the superb Scottish educational system and another ten from Canada. Given extra time to study, these two groups were passing the actuarial exams at a rapid clip. Unfortunately management was having trouble finding duties worthy of these men's talents. That left no room whatsoever for another student in the program, especially one who had failed to live up to his potential. In a word I had screwed myself.

Still, I had not done poor office work. I had been conscientious to a fault and was now in charge of a substantial section of the actuarial division. But it was a dead-end job and I knew it. My boss was a full-fledged actuary. The best I could ever expect would be a minor, nondescript, supervisory position. Something had to be done.

Since the company could not be expected to reinstate me as an actuarial student, I had no other choice but to study for the exams on my own time. The first step was obvious: to obtain associate standing with the Society of Actuaries. That would give me the right to put A.S.A. (Associate Society of Actuaries) after my name. To secure my A.S.A., I had to pass eight exams. I passed the first four exams without cracking a book since they entailed math I had had at McGill. The other four exams were different having been designed wholly for application to insurance. The exams were held in early spring with the results made public late in 1933. I decided to take two exams in the spring of 1935 and 1936. That would give me a start, generate a modest pay hike, and allow me to contemplate marriage. Admittedly my place on the "actuarial ladder" would not be as good as several other men who had taken the program seriously. But at least my position would be secure. I could then concentrate on the last four exams, the ones needed to become the scarcest of insurance beasts: a full fellow with the right to affix the initials F.S.A. (Fellow of the Society of Actuaries) after my name.

Chapter 15

LE BELLE DAME SANS MERCI

The Beautiful Lady Without Mercy

I kept none of this secret from Marcelle but not until Labor Day 1934 did I spell out my plans in detail.

"I need to start studying for the actuarial exams," I said. "Since my office work leaves me no time to study on company time, I will only be able to see you a couple of nights a week and possibly on Saturday or Sunday afternoon. Can you handle that?"

"Of course I can," she said brightly. "The last thing I want is to stunt your career. No, I will be perfectly happy. You know how much I love being with my mother and my sisters."

"Good," I said.

Then Marcelle said something odd.

"Anyway, Madeleine will soon tire of Reggie. I just know it. Surely she can't be foolish enough to spend the rest of her life with that man."

Ah, there it was again: Marcelle's great fantasy. Madeleine would grow weary of Reggie and come bouncing back to me– as if I wanted Reggie Molson's leavings! Here Marcelle was totally out of sync with the other members of her family. She firmly believed that her sister would get over her infatuation and return to the Hudon fold. Then it happened. Madeleine eloped and married Reggie. Marcelle was both shocked and disgusted.

"How could my sister do such an abominable thing?" she said. "I don't cry easily but the last few nights I have had to cry myself to sleep. Madeleine is lost, irrevocably lost. Why, she doesn't even live in Montreal any more. Reggie has moved his mother to Florida and you know what that means."

I tried to console her but it wasn't any good. There are psychic things that go on between twins that the rest of humanity does not understand.

Not being directly involved, I can only guess what had happened. Through her work with a prominent brokerage firm, Lucille knew the scions of several wealthy Montreal families, two being Reggie and his brother. Along with Mrs. Hudon she also took a motherly interest in her twin sisters. As years passed Madeleine became more and more pliant to Reggie's will. Lucille could not help but notice that Madeleine had not only lost all her girlfriends but also dressed in clothes more befitting an old maid. More ominously, though Reggie preferred Marcelle to Madeleine, he did not hesitate to exploit Madeleine's love for him.

This Lucille could not countenance. Meeting Reggie privately, she issued an ultimatum.

"Listen, Reggie," she said. "Either marry Madeleine or leave her alone."

"Lucille, this is really none of your business. Your sister is of age and can make her own decisions."

"Oh, is she now? That's not the way I see it. Madeleine is young and beautiful and needs to be out with men her age, men who can properly appreciate her. Instead, she is mooning over you while you pursue Marcelle. That has got to stop."

"And just how do you intend to stop it?"

"Here's how. Just how long do you think Marcelle or even Madeleine would have anything to do with you if I spilt the beans?"

"What beans?"

"Don't be coy. You know exactly what I'm talking about. You were not always thirty-nine years old. In your twenties you were quite the gay young blade and catted around this town something fierce. I even have the names of some of your flames if you don't believe me."

"Are you trying to blackmail me?"

"No, just warning you that I will pass on the information."

"You wouldn't dare."

"Wouldn't I? Just try me. The twins are my sisters, Reggie. Never forget that."

No one from the Hudon family was invited to the wedding–not even Mrs. Hudon. Reggie was wily about that. On the way to Florida with his mother and Madeleine, he had arranged a stopover in Washington, D.C. There, in early December 1934, Reginald Owen Molson took Madeleine Hudon to wife at an undisclosed location.[15]

Clearly Reggie was piqued. I did not really know him until after he had married Madeleine. His hatred for Lucille bordered on the pathological. He never referred to her by name. Instead, he called her "Fat Ass" and, to my knowledge, would have nothing to do with her. For her part Lucille didn't seem to care. She had protected her sister. That was all that mattered to her.

Madeleine's departure drew Marcelle and me closer together. I loved her more and more and did not hesitate to articulate my love. But I could never get her to say she loved me. Nevertheless, that did not worry me. She was now wearing my fraternity pin, so clearly I was her boyfriend.

The New Year's Eve of 1935 was so delightful I decided to start a diary. I only made a few entries, however, but these have somehow survived the ravages of time. I print them here for one reason only: to show the wonders of young love:

Tuesday: January 1, 1935

Easily the best New Year's Eve I ever had. Spent the evening alone with Marcelle listening to the radio and playing Ping Pong. I love her more than I ever thought I could love anyone. There is every reason for hoping that at last I have found my complement. She's so beautiful and wonderful though that I cannot believe she could ever love a person so unworthy as I am. I left her place shortly after two a.m. and on arriving home went straight to bed.

I got up about 11 and Dad and I went to Krausmann's for dinner. We proceeded from there to the Palace– Shirley Temple in *Bright Eyes*, a punk show, but on the whole we had a great time. From there Dad went home and I trotted up to Marcelle's with a view to going to another show. This, however, was not to be for Gertrude was down from Ottawa to see my love. We waved good-bye to her at the train station (10:15 p.m.). Walked back in the blizzard to Murray's. There we had coffee and decided that I should pass part 3 and 5– only three evenings and one afternoon per week to see each other for a while. We

---

[15] This part of the memoir should be taken with a grain of salt. Both the author's speculations concerning Lucille and Reggie and Madeleine's nuptials in Washington, D.C.–if that indeed was the locale–have as yet to be verified.

talked marriage in June 1936. Oh! I hope and pray it will be so. I love her! I love her!

Bed @ 12:15.

Wednesday: January 2, 1935

Got up as usual and proceeded to the office. The day was quiet and in the evening I went with Marcelle to the Strand. We saw *College Tour* and *Pursuit of Happiness*, an indifferent show but I love Marcelle so it was enjoyable. Had coffee at Murray's and then went home.

Bed at 12:30 a.m.

Thursday: January 3, 1935

Got up and went to the office as usual. This afternoon Bill told me that he might be transferred to the Policy Department and that I would take his old position as head of the Change Section. I dropped in to see Mr. Cunningham, and he confirmed Bill's story and told me to work hard at my studies. He's a peach. Afterwards I dropped in on Art and he said some nice things. This made me so excited that I had the jitters all evening. I lost a night that I should have studied. By God! I'll make it up or bust; and that's no fooling. I went to the office right after supper and just wasted the evening, bowling six strings alone and then coming home to bridge. I phoned My Darling and told her the news. She was very pleased and wished me the best. I guess I'll go to bed now hoping for the best.

Another blizzard today– bed at 11:30 p.m.

That spring I passed two actuarial exams, and Marcelle and I celebrated accordingly. That summer we had a swell time in the old Model A before I resumed my studies in September. Still, I did not press my suit. Though now intimate companions, I never once kissed her good night. An invisible fence seemed to surround her.

Towards summer's end my neat little world fell apart. Marcelle and I were spending most evenings driving around in the Model A or just taking advantage of the summer weather to go for leisurely strolls. At her doorstep one evening in late August she dropped the bomb.

"I believe we are seeing too much of one another," she blurted out. "It might be healthier for us to date others for a spell."

I was thunderstruck.

"I-I don't get it," I said finally. "I was under the impression that we had an understanding, a very deep and sincere commitment to each other."

"We are dear, dear friends," she said sheepishly. "And I want us to stay that way. But I need more space. I need to be free to date other men."

I was floored but what could I do?

"Listen, Marcelle. You know that I love you far too much to be just a casual friend. I can't force you to love me but I can't live a lie either."

And with that I turned and walked away, crushed.

64   Leavings

Dick and Marcelle Christmas on their honeymoon in Val-Morin in early October 1936.

Christmas Family Collection

Chapter 16

PIECE JUSTIFICATIVE
Justificatory Paper

After agonizing about the situation for a couple of days, I went to my desk and wrote Marcelle a lengthy letter. It was the most difficult letter of my life. It wasn't a love letter exactly. Rather it spelled out my deepest feeling and ideals, the noble goals that I had expected from our love and that were now lost forever. Marcelle kept this letter for her entire life. By chance our younger son Gerry found it in a shoebox at our home in Rochester, New York. The letter is here presented exactly as I wrote it:

Early spring 1935

Dear Marcelle:

    When you think that the problem, which this week has presented to me, has been such that on no night have I had more than four hours sleep and last night I had not a wink, it is understandable that an analysis of, and possibility of solution of it, presents great difficulties.

    In the first place I wish to apologize for our farewell last night. When I look back on it, I can see that it was but a feeble effort to create a straw by a man who could feel the waters of despair close over his head. I appreciate the strength on your part in insuring that I be completely drowned. The following, though brief, is an honest effort to explain my views on the subject and I hope you will view them with gentle understanding because I still believe you to be kind.

    I am quite willing to keep on seeing you if you get into the habit again of going with other fellows, provided of course that the basis of our comradeship changes. For at the best, under those circumstances, we could only be friends and any possibility of what I understand "love" to mean would be quite out of the question.

By this I would convey that I loved you up until Monday night. Of course, since that time an idiot could see there had been no love between us, for we have not even acted as friends. In the future, however, there seems to be no reason why we shouldn't be good friends.

I want you to understand what I mean by "love." When we really started going about together just a year ago, you were going around with several fellows at the same time. Love to me, then, did not exist. It was not until the early fall when you said good-bye to the others and I became your only and therefore much closer companion in very nearly all your spare time that love began to come to me. For it was only then that our friendship developed that intimacy which enabled you to reveal (not only by talking, but by your actions) just what your hopes, fears and ambitions were. As the revelation of your personality gradually unfolded itself, I became entranced with the sweetness and preciousness of your dear self, and I thought I could see a place for myself in those hopes of yours. So your hopes and ambitions became my hopes and ambitions and I vowed that I would do everything in my power to bring the loveliness you envisioned to fulfillment. All these precious things were bound up within you so that you became the one thing necessary to all that I held dear and worthwhile in life.

This growth was very gradual because you are not casually intimate. It must be remembered that for eight or nine months this constant companionship existed in which we shared thoughts that were voiced to no others. In those months when I was your only intimate pal and you were mine, you grew to become of the most precious part of my life. In other words, according to my understanding, I learnt to "love" you.

I am not entirely to blame for this because you gave me some indications that my love was not misplaced. Otherwise, I never would have let my dreams blend so completely into yours. It was you, after all, who made our intimate companionship possible by discouraging your other suitors early last fall. What was more important you admitted as we went along that you were very fond of me and felt that you were growing fonder and fonder which from you is a real admission. I was gloriously happy.

Then suddenly, utterly without warning, you casually convey to me that you wanted to go back to the stage where I was to be one of many boys, who would keep *steady* company with you and share those thoughts and hopes of yours, which blessed privilege you had given exclusively to me and from which had grown my great love for you. To say I was stunned is to put it mildly. It is evident that the hopes and dreams that we shared were ours exclusively just as long as they were shared with no others. In other words the real you cannot be the most important part of me as well as the most important parts of others. What you asked of me was to give up that love for you that had grown slowly and yet was so strong and precious and *go back* and play the part of the casual friend, the one of many, that I was last summer. Oh! Can't you see the difference? Last summer I was actually the casual boyfriend, but this spring I had become the lover. So don't you think for a moment that it was an easy thing you asked of me to do on Monday.

However, I think I have succeeded in granting your wish. Once you insisted on seeing others, you condemned my love. That is what has hurt me so terribly this week. You, without warning, asked me to put my love aside and become a casual friend. The suffering that I have passed through has been the killing of that love which I once felt sure would never die. So now, it's over. I feel sure I can safely say that you can see whom you will (myself included if you wish), when you will and why you will. All that has happened is that the question of love between us is (and for a long time in the future will be) dead.

Perhaps my conception of love is too lofty, but I have always hitched wagons to stars.

Sincerely,
Dick

My break with Marcelle did not cause me to drop my plans regarding the actuarial examinations. I needed something to do, something to stop myself from wallowing in self-pity. Developments in the communist and fascist countries had led me to believe that neither held the answer to humanity's woes. In fact, our broad-based political democracy with its free enterprise economic system was vastly superior to either of them. I had reached the startling conclusion that the many ills affecting society had their origin in humans themselves and could only be eliminated by the insertion of a higher ethical and moral code– the operation of Darwinian evolution being far too slow.

I found out later why Marcelle had acted in the bizarre way she did. A Scot in the Investment Department had the hots for her. Getting Mrs. Hudon on the line, he had engaged her in a spirited conversation in which they were both adept. When Mrs. Hudon divined the purpose of the young man's call, she readily encouraged his suit. Along with a number of other people Mrs. Hudon did not consider me to be a suitable mate for Marcelle. The Scot would therefore lurk in the shadows of Marcelle's home until we had said goodnight. Upon my departure he would emerge, knock on the door, and be admitted by Mrs. Hudon. The Scot would then chitchat with Marcelle and her mother. Eventually Marcelle would excuse herself and go to bed. But the Scot would banter with Mrs. Hudon–a notorious night owl–for another hour or two afterwards. This went on for weeks. Finally the Scot was able to wrangle a date with Marcelle.

A month passed. One night I received a friendly phone call from Jeanne.

"Where have you been keeping yourself?" she said coyly. "We are all worried about you, especially Marcelle. She might appreciate a call from you."

I tried to sound non-committal with Jeanne but am sure she could see right through me.

The next night I telephoned Marcelle. Not wanting to mention a word about our breakup, I got straight to the point.

"I have some free-time this weekend. How would you like to go out?"

"I'd love to," she said.

We immediately took up from where we left off only now we talked about "we" rather than "I." Unwittingly the Scot had done me a huge favor.

I never found out what happened between Marcelle and the Scot. That remained a taboo subject throughout our married life. Being a Scot, he probably made a lame pass at her, which she firmly rebuked. Marcelle was so sexy-looking and certainly did not contemplate the sex act with repugnance. But she was a woman with incredible high ethical and moral standards. Though not religious, she was spiritual in the strictest sense of the word. Her body and her mind were for her to give, not for a man to take.

I passed the two actuarial exams on schedule. Now I was an associate in the Society of Actuaries. This brought an automatic promotion to "Chief Clerk," a euphemism for being an actuarial assistant. More importantly I no longer had to eat with the peons and punch silly time cards. Instead, I ate in a special dining room and had such goodies as a key to the men's restroom.

Around this time Marcelle and I adopted the bizarre habit of walking about in furniture stores. Here, she was in her element: shopping or at least pretending to shop. Early on in our courtship I had figured out that shopping gave her great happiness. I did not know that it would become a lifelong passion.

I never did propose directly to Marcelle. Both being shy our engagement was something that evolved over time. We nonetheless set a date–October 1, 1936–as the day we would tie the knot. We next went "house hunting." We found an apartment that was perfect for us.

I was aglow with happiness. My long and arduous courtship was about to be consummated despite numerous setbacks, the worst being the death of my mother in 1934. My father was not only terribly lonesome after her death but also in desperate financial straits. One day he took me aside.

"Son, I have met a woman named Caroline Henderson. She's a spinster around my age. We have decided to get married."

"That's great, Dad. I'm very happy for you."

"I'm glad you understand. Louise and Alan are really upset about it. They are young and don't understand how lonely I am. I want you to know that no one will ever take the place of your mother. She was the love of my life."

The world was faring even worse than my father. My friends and I watched in horror as "the great democracies" allowed Hitler and Mussolini to suppress the partisans in the Spanish Civil War. A "Canadian brigade" was formed and sent to Spain to assist the Spanish partisans. For a moment I was tempted to join but Marcelle dissuaded me, thank God. A couple of my friends died fighting with their bare hands.

Though my friends thought Marcelle and I were mismatched, our families shared many similarities. Both the Hudons and the Christmases were not Johnny-come-latelies. Each family was well respected in Montreal: the Hudons amongst the French Canadians and our family amongst the English Canadians. Granted, Marcelle and I came from branches of our respective families that were far from affluent. But that did not stop us from being proud, from holding solid middle-class values, from demanding respect.

Our wedding was a simple one as befitted our circumstances and our desires. It took place in a small chapel,[16] for in those days a protestant was not allowed to marry a Catholic in the church. Only members of our immediate families were in attendance. After the ceremony the reception was held at the Hudon apartment. Marcelle was dressed in traveling clothes throughout and looked adorable. I was deliriously happy.

We left the Hudon apartment about 10 p.m. and took off for our apartment in the Model A. There, we spent the night unbeknownst to anyone. The following morning we drove to our cottage in Val-Morin where we were alone, as the summer residents had long departed. The weather was ideal, and we played golf and boated at our leisure. Then we woke up one morning to find it snowing quite hard, so we jumped into the trusty Model A and took off for home. We spent the balance of our two-week honeymoon lounging about the apartment.

---

[16] On October 1, 1936 Dick and Marcelle were married in the chapel at St. Jacques Cathedral in Montreal. Not being allowed to marry in the cathedral so infuriated Marcelle that she would subsequently break with the church despite having been educated by nuns.

Albert Hudon in later life (circa 1940)
Christmas Family Collection

Chapter 17

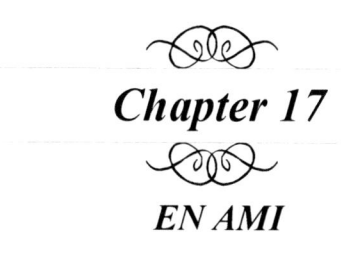

EN AMI

As a Friend

Marcelle and I soon learned that we had a male "fairy godmother"– Uncle Albert Hudon. He not only influenced several vital decisions but also through his generosity made it possible for me to join the Royal Canadian Navy.

Uncle Albert left home at the age of fifteen. There appears to be no particular reason for his departure. He just felt the time had come for him to strike out on his own. It was an excellent decision. From the outset he exhibited astonishing business acumen. He not only displayed an ability to make money but, like the Molsons, had the right good sense to keep it. In 1950 he left an estate valued at twelve million dollars and during his lifetime had contributed to many different charities. Clearly he was a man of great sagacity, industry, and foresight.

Uncle Albert had a few idiosyncrasies, all being innocuous. First, he was obsessed with "blood." He had married twice but was childless. He therefore doted on his nieces and nephews and openly declared that at his death his estate would be distributed amongst them, with specific provisions being made for his widow's upkeep and charities that were near and dear to his heart. This fascination for "blood" manifested itself in other ways. Hearing through Mrs. Hudon that I liked the twins, for instance, he immediately telephoned my father.

"This is marvelous," he said. "There is good blood on each side."

Yet another idiosyncrasy of Uncle Albert was his fascination in solidly built older houses. He got a kick out of carefully examining a house that was up for sale. If he found the house to be structurally sound and the asking price low, he would then buy it and give it to one of his nieces and nephews. This was how Marcelle and I secured our first house, the one on Western Avenue right after Bill was born. What a birthday gift!

In 1940 Uncle Albert formed an investment company called the Dollard Company. To get the company up and running, Albert had to donate securities to generate common stock for various family members. Marcelle's share was twenty-five thousand dollars – not a paltry sum in those days. As a result, Marcelle had this nest egg as well as a house when I joined the Royal Canadian Navy, an act that Albert wholeheartedly approved.

Uncle Albert's avowed intent with the Dollard Company was simple: to teach the male heads of the family how to handle investments. These individuals formed the company's Board of Directors and met monthly with him. It was a splendid idea on paper but failed miserably in practice– not because Albert made a mistake but because the other male heads lacked the inclination and drive to make the enterprise succeed. The failure of the Dollard Company made me realize that we cannot strive too hard against peoples' natural inclinations and interests. People gravitate to their own instinctual drives. It's as simple as that.

76   *Leavings*

Marcelle and Bill Christmas in their duplex on McLynn Avenue in Westmount, Quebec (1940). Dick almost surely took this picture. He always said that Marcelle was at the height of her beauty with children.

Christmas Family Collection

Chapter 18

AU MIEUX

On Intimate terms

Marcelle and I were delectably happy the two years we spent in the apartment. We were young and healthy and had loads of friends, most of whom were couples of our age. Sure, we were poor by today's standards but so were all our friends! I decided to take a sabbatical year from actuarial studies and upon resuming them the following year passed the first two parts of the fellowship examinations. Our financial situation now seemed secure, especially with Marcelle in line to inherit a considerable amount of money when Uncle Albert died. We therefore decided to start a family.

At the end of two years we moved into a duplex on McLynn Avenue. Ours was a newly built one. It had three bedrooms, two being tiny at best. So I used one for a study. The entire block consisted of duplexes occupied by couples like us. Our circle of friends was therefore even wider than before. Marcelle became pregnant almost immediately. I decided to take yet another sabbatical to help her with her pregnancy. That turned out to be one of the biggest mistakes of my life for reasons neither of us could foresee.

Billy was born on June 5, 1939. With her deep maternal instincts Marcelle quickly blossomed into a superb mother. I loved taking pictures of her and the baby as her face just glowed with happiness.

Later that year Canada, being a British Dominion, was at war. A world war poses many problems for a life insurance company, especially an international institution like the Sun Life. As fate would have it, I worked in the department where most of these difficulties were located. It was therefore impossible for me to study like I had in the past. As a result, I barely missed passing the last two fellowship exams in the spring of 1940. I was shocked for I had never failed an actuarial exam before.

It really wasn't fair, not fair at all. I had competed against American students whose country was not at war. Usually Canadians did better than their American counterparts, but not that year. Indeed, in 1940 not one Canadian student passed either part. I was really upset. My only consolation was that I had come the closest. But "coming the closest" doesn't count for much in life.

Months went by. One day Dad called me on the phone from his office and asked me to fetch a taxi, as he wasn't feeling well. My stepmother and I then walked over to the office to see what was wrong. Upon our arrival Dad was sitting in a chair holding his coat and hat. He looked dreadful and had the strangest expression on his face. I'm no doctor, but my guess was he had suffered a heart attack. I helped him to his feet, took him down the stairs, and hailed a passing taxi. On the way back home we passed the Royal Victoria Hospital. I immediately suggested we go there. My stepmother would have none of it.

"I want him home in his little bed where I can take care of him," she said.

So home we went. Home was a modest apartment on the third floor. That, I believe, was our undoing. The taxi driver was a great guy and helped me assist Dad up the stairs. It seemed to take forever. At one point Dad turned to me and said, "Son, I've never felt this tired in my life."

After getting Dad into his "little bed," I called the doctor who promised to come immediately. Not long afterwards Dad had a second attack– this one a killer. My stepmother became hysterical. The doctor arrived forty-five minutes later and pronounced him dead.

"Where on earth have you been?" I asked.

"I'm sorry," he replied. "I was delayed on my way with an emergency."

I was thunderstruck. God gave my father many gifts and many talents. Luck, however, was not one of them.

With the onslaught of World War II, I discovered I was "snake bit," that I was still vitally interested in the human race. I also discovered that I was better informed than my contemporaries. For the most part they had swallowed the pap of the propagandists. I had not. I had become a male Cassandra with all the woe that entails. Yet my thoughts and visions did not give me the right to involve those nearest and dearest to me, especially my beloved Marcelle and our newborn son.

Having read *Mein Kemp,* I had no illusions about Hitler. He was a mad dog, plain and simple. If the Establishment via the modern media had its way, Hitler would be its paranoiac vehicle with which to destroy the archenemy: communism. Yes, as far as the Establishment was concerned, the Soviet Union was the real foe, not Nazi Germany. The "Great Democracies" proved that over and over again with their appeasement policies from 1931 on. Then Hitler overreached himself and bombed Poland in September 1939. Having a treaty with Poland, Great Britain and France had no other choice but to declare war. That or grant Hitler what he wanted: world domination.

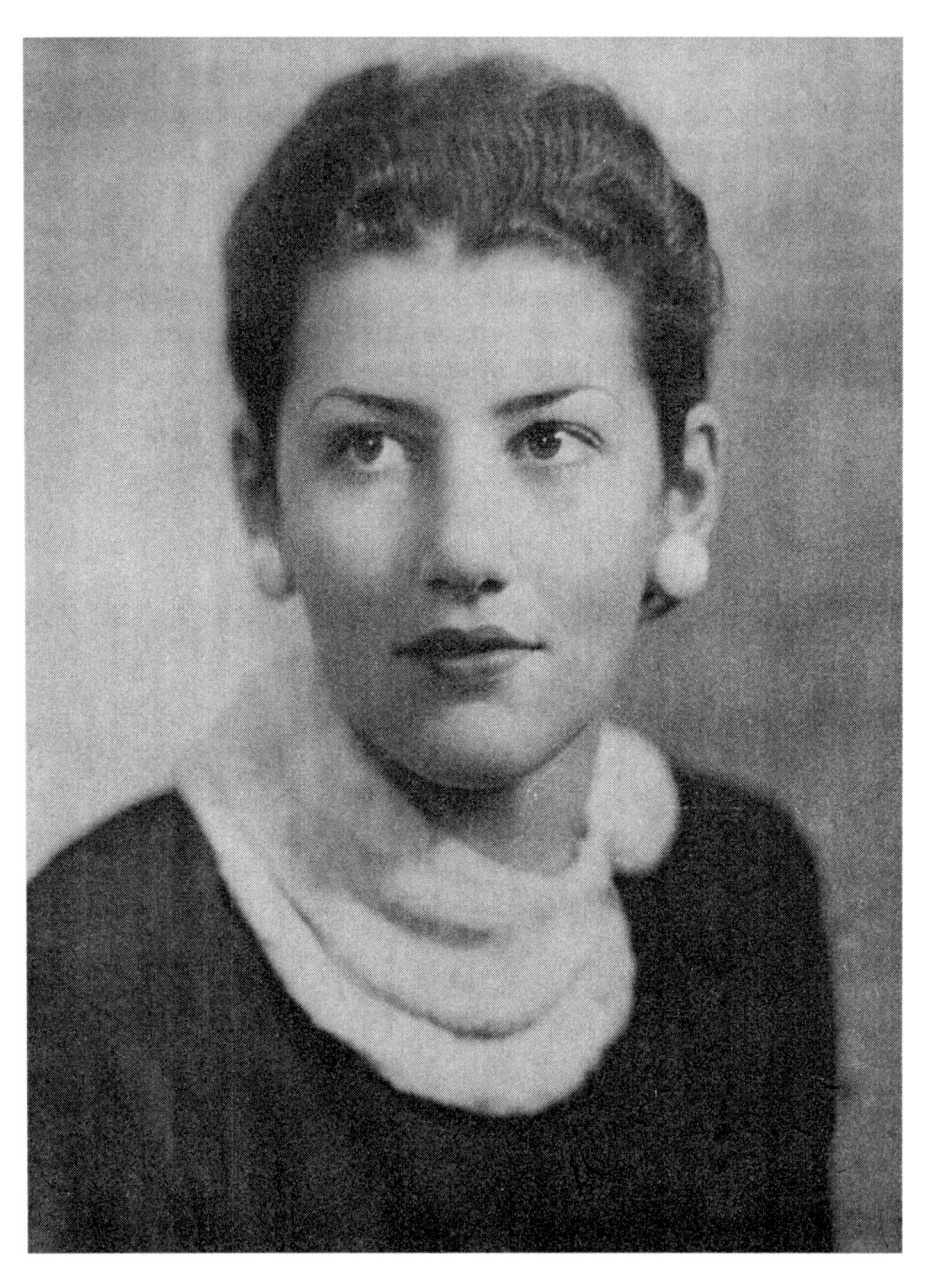

Dick's sister Louise during World War II. Divorced from her husband just prior to the war, Louise would subsequently remarry Dick Walkem and have two wonderful children, Mary Louise "Flicka" and George.

Christmas Family Collection

Chapter 19

GUERRE A OUTRANCE
War to the Uttermost

British and French soldiers were unprepared to do battle against Hitler's crack armies. Nonetheless, they felt impregnable behind the Mignot Line where they sang such nonsense as "we're hanging up our washing on the Siegfried Line"– the German fortifications just opposite theirs. Establishment-controlled radio and newspapers labeled this "the Phony War" hoping against hope that Hitler would come to his senses and be reasonable. Individuals such as myself knew the phrase "the Phony War" for what it was– a sham. That became clear in the spring of 1940 when the Germans blitzkrieged France in a mere six weeks and Great Britain escaped a similar fate more by geography than by good management. Thanks to the heroics of the RAF, the Luftwaffe failed to wrest control of the air over the English Channel. It was a near thing, much nearer than most historians care to admit. Churchill had it right when he said it was the RAF's "finest hour."

With great reluctance Hitler had to acknowledge that he could not conquer Great Britain with bombs alone. But Britain had never been his chief adversary. Russia was. Fearful that the Russians under Joe Stalin would fully mobilize for war, Hitler came to the conclusion that the sooner he attacked Russia the better. In June 1941 the German armies invaded Russia. Until winter set in, conventional wisdom held that the Germans had the upper hand, the assumption being that, once Moscow fell, Russia was doomed.

As expected, the media used propaganda to obscure the desperate situation the Allies faced in Europe. There was genuine fear that the public morale in Canada would be shattered with another German victory. This was particularly true in Quebec where there were so many French Canadian Catholics. Seeing France fall, many French Canadians thought Canada had chosen the wrong side. Then, when

Mussolini joined forces with Hitler soon afterwards, French Canadians were doubly vexed. And who could blame them? How could they wholeheartedly support a war against a country that housed the Vatican? Furthermore, why should they embrace atheistic Russia over Catholic Italy? Indeed pro-Fascist sentiment ran so high in Quebec that the mayor of Montreal[17] had to be incarcerated in a detention camp for his opposition to the draft. As a result, Canada was a house divided at a critical moment in world history.

Due to knowledge gleaned from books before the war, I could foresee major events well before they happened. I therefore found myself out-of-step with public opinion, particularly with business associates. Soon I had postulated Christmas' Law on Executives and Warfare: *the loftier the senior executive the farther removed from the realities of war.* Around the office I therefore tried to keep my mouth shut. Still, that hardly kept my mind off the war. I was not surprised with the fall of France but held out hope that the British navy and the RAF could keep the Germans at bay. Canadian newspapers said otherwise with a constant drumbeat on the invincibility of the Luftwaffe. Needless to say I "sweated blood" all through the Battle of Britain.

The U-boat warfare that followed wasn't much better. Stretching well into 1942 and sinking vessels faster than they could be replaced, these U-boats begged the question: how long could Great Britain maintain a beachhead should the time ever come for the Allies to mount a counteroffensive? For if Great Britain were to fall even the combined effort of the United States and Canada could not stop Hitler from conquering the world.

These fears were not removed when Hitler invaded Russia, and the United States was forced into the fray with the Japanese bombing of Pearl Harbor on December 7, 1941. Of course, I was delighted that the United States had now entered the war, but the Japanese had the Americans on the ropes until the Battle of Midway swung things the other way in June 1942.

As the war progressed, I felt more and more the need to serve, to do my bit. This would disrupt my career. But what was a career if Hitler prevailed? Terribly divided, I decided to have a talk with

---

[17] Camillien Houde (1889 - 1958), four-time mayor of Montreal. In 1940 Houde was arrested and charged under the Defense of Canada Regulations. He was imprisoned at Camp Petawawa in Ontario until the end of the war.

Marcelle. If anyone could steer me aright, she could. After laying my cards on the table, I sat back and waited for her response.

"I did not marry a man of war," she said evenly. "But I did marry a man of principle, a man who cannot sit back and watch evil win. But then there's your age and then there's our child. I don't want to be a widow. I don't want our son to grow up fatherless."

"Then you think I should stay out of it."

"I did not say that," she said bravely. "I was just telling you *my* fears."

"I guess the question comes down to this: what can we do? What can a couple in our circumstances contribute to the war effort?"

"Yes, that would seem to sum it up."

"Well, I could join the militia. That way I would be of service and still be safe. But I would have to take a huge cut in pay. Can you live on less?"

"You know I can," she said. "I've lived on less for most of my life."

So I joined the militia, the final defense should the Germans ever invade us. What a pathetic hodgepodge of guys! We met only once a week and the equipment was, at best, World War I vintage.

Thus matters stood for months. Then someone high up in the militia discovered my technical knowledge in math and physics and offered me the rank of full lieutenant in anti-U-boat warfare. Of course I should have paid no heed to the offer. The war had started to swing in the favor of the Allies, and I could therefore expect a sunny future with the Sun Life. Without exception the married actuaries my age avoided service like the plague. This was particularly true of the imported Scots. If anyone used the war for personal advancement at the Sun Life, those sly whiz kids did.

Again, I decided to talk with Marcelle– an inexcusable act that only gave greater credence to Mrs. Hudon's belief that I was not a suitable mate.

"Joining the navy might adversely affect my position in the Sun Life after the war," I said. "That is a great risk."

"That risk is nothing when compared to the thought of you being killed. I will have to live with that fear every day you are away from me."

I bit my lip.

"But what kind of a life would you have and what kind of a life would our son have in a world run by a madman?"

Marcelle said nothing for a long, long time. She just looked at me with those soft, sky-blue eyes.

"I can't do it alone," she said finally. "I'm not strong enough for it. Just sitting here in the apartment alone with the baby day after day after day would be too much for me."

"Well," I said. "What if I could arrange for my sister Louise to stay here in my place? Louise, as you know, is a gay divorcee now."

"All right," she said reluctantly. "If you can get Louise to keep me company, you can go. Just come back in one piece. Don't do anything stupid."

Louise readily agreed. Her ex-husband, Dick Walkem, was a military man, a graduate from RMC (Royal Military Academy). Being a colonel in an active reserve regiment, Dick had enlisted the day war had been declared. He was still madly in love with Louise and bombarded her with letters begging for reconciliation. Eventually he won out. After the war Dick and Louise remarried and had two children: Mary Louise "Flicka" and George.

Louise teaming up with Marcelle worked like a charm. I suppose Billy can vaguely remember the bond he had with "Auntie Toe"– his nickname for her, one that stuck for life.

When the U-boats were finally brought under control in early 1945, I brought Marcelle and our two sons–Gerry being born on January 2, 1944–to Ottawa where I was now stationed. Discharged with he rank of lieutenant commander in late 1945, I gathered the family together, returned to Montreal, and resumed civilian life.

At the Sun Life I found that the smart people were those who had stood fast to avoid service in the armed forces. Sure, I was given "my old job back," but the others had forged ahead in my absence. The Sun Life is not to be faulted for this. In the business world it is unavoidable, save for a few exceptions. I could not expect to be one of these exceptions having broken so many rules in the past. I had one huge asset, however. Soon after the war I had passed the last of my actuarial exams. I was now a professionally qualified actuary (F.S.A.). Since actuaries were scarcer than hens' teeth in the United States, I had another powwow with Marcelle.

"The big question for us," she said sadly, "is our families. Mine is shrinking fast. Mother, Lucille, Alain, and Geraldine have moved to Vancouver. Madeleine is without a country traveling the way she does with Reggie. That just leaves Jeanne and Gerard, the two we socialize with the least."

"My situation is even worse. Both my parents are dead; Louise has remarried Dick Walkem and is now living in Vancouver; and my kid brother Alan is in Toronto. That makes me the last survivor of my nuclear family here in Montreal."

"But if we move to the States," Marcelle said, "I don't want to be far from home. New England would probably be best for us."

I agreed and started to send out feelers.

86   Leavings

Dick, Bill, Marcelle, and Gerry Christmas on the steps of their duplex at 4842 Western Avenue (now DeMaisonneuve) towards the end of World War II (1944). This was the duplex that Uncle Albert inspected and bought for them. Auntie May resided in an identical unit next door.

Christmas Family Collection

PART TWO

Springfield

Bill, Marcelle, and Gerry (a.k.a. "Little Jud) Christmas shortly before they left Montréal to live on Rogers Avenue in West Springfield, Massachusetts (1945).

Christmas Family Collection

Chapter 20

A BRAS OUVERTS

With Open Arms

The unsavory situation at the Sun Life was not the sole spur that prompted me to seek employment in the United States. Trouble was brewing between the French-speaking and the English-speaking citizens that would one day lead to out-and-out bloodshed. Having two boys did not make that an attractive situation. To emphasize matters, the mayor of Montreal had been incarcerated in a detention center for openly supporting the fascist powers during the World War II. Upon his release from prison he was accorded the greatest hero's welcome in the city's history. Talk about handwriting on the wall! Only a fool, if free to find employment elsewhere, would stay in such an environment. Years later, while visiting Montreal, I found all my fears justified. The English-speakers in the city had a haggard, beaten look about them. Clearly they had lost the culture war and were now paying the price. Montreal was now predominantly French in both language and customs. I was shocked to see that even the street on which we had once lived had been renamed: Western Avenue was now Maisoneuve Avenue.

Fortunately during the decade following World War II I was able to secure almost any executive position I wanted. I was not only a fully qualified professional with plenty of experience but also extremely gregarious in comparison to my fellow actuaries. Most actuaries are introspective and are therefore viewed as "cold fish." I even had a fellow actuary once say to me: "You can't be an actuary. I actually enjoy talking with you."

Gerry Hill reported to me at the Sun Life. A gold medalist in math and physics from Queen's College, Gerry was ten years my junior. Studying for the actuarial exams after the war, he noticed that Canadian-born students were not getting a square deal in their native country. He thought this was patently unfair. Meanwhile, I had made a survey of actuaries in several U.S. companies. This survey revealed that U.S. companies of similar size and services as the Sun Life had far fewer actuaries.

"I can't believe my eyes," Gerry said. "Your data is stunning, absolutely stunning. And I'm going to act on it. Being from Toronto, I have no ties to this joint."

"My hands are tied right now," I said. "I still have six weeks before my discharge goes through. Still, I will talk to Marcelle and see if she is not adverse to the idea."

Gerry landed a job with the Massachusetts Mutual Life Insurance Company in a matter of weeks. "My God!" I said to myself. "Are actuaries ever in demand in the U.S. I'd better strike while the iron is hot."

The demand was even hotter than I thought. I wrote a letter to Gerry in Springfield, Massachusetts asking for advice on how to proceed. Before Gerry could reply, I received a long distant phone call from John Miller, the vice-president and chief actuary at the Monarch Life Insurance Company.

"Hello, Dick," he said. "This is John Miller at the Monarch. I was having lunch with Gerry Hill yesterday, and he said that you were on the loose. Mr. Hill spoke most favorably about you and said that you might be interested in relocating to the United States. To be perfectly frank, I'm in desperate need of another actuary to act as my assistant. Would you like to come down for an interview?"

Well, your mother and I went to Springfield and received the red carpet treatment. We liked everything we saw. Your mother particularly liked the easy driving distance to and from Montreal. We stayed over a day to spend some time with Gerry and his wife Marge.

"The Monarch is much smaller than either the Sun Life or the Mass Mutual," he said. "It nevertheless has a great reputation around here for being a happy company. What are they offering you?"

"Much more money than I'm receiving now and John looks like he would be a great boss. If Marcelle doesn't have any objections, I'm going to accept the position."

Marcelle did not have any objections. The six and a half years in Springfield were the happiest ones of my life. Our ages and the ages of you two boys were contributing factors to this happiness but not the only ones. We had been told to beware of New Englanders, that they were aloof if not downright hostile to newcomers. We found that, though true of "down-Easters," it certainly was not applicable with our new neighbors on Rogers Avenue in West Springfield. They welcomed us with open arms, and we soon had a flock of friends.

I came to view the world as my oyster. Though now in my forties, I felt that Marcelle and I could go anywhere in the United States and meet with the same loving affection we had in Springfield. Talk about a horse's ass!

Gerry and Marge Hill became our nearest and dearest friends. That relationship was further consolidated when in 1948 I left the Monarch to the join the Mass Mutual. Being right across the street from each other, the two companies had an unwritten agreement not to swap personnel. But a position opened up in the Mass Mutual that I could not pass up. So one day I cleared out my desk, said good-bye to my friends at the Monarch, and walked across the street to begin my new job.

My new job gave me a free hand directing the new group line under Harry Pierce, the company's executive VP. Pierce was a law unto himself. The only person in the company with more power and prestige was the president, Alex MacLean. Pierce and MacLean had made Gerry their fair-haired boy, the darling of the company. Everyone assumed Gerry would be the next president. As is often the case when two able individuals run a company, they belatedly realize that they are mortal. This is what happened to Pierce and MacLean. Approaching the mandatory retirement age of sixty-five, Alex had hoped Harry–five years his junior–would take his place. Harry wanted none of it. He was perfectly happy being executive VP, the power behind the throne.

But Pierce found himself in a quandary. In those days it was unthinkable for a man under the age of forty to head a major insurance company like the Mass Mutual. And Gerry was still in his thirties! The Mass Mutual field agents were an elite group, an exclusive club of millionaires. Everyone to a man was in his fifties or early sixties. There was no way that these men would listen to Gerry Hill, let alone follow him. Maybe they would ten or fifteen years hence but not now. So MacLean and Pierce did the logical thing: they hired an outsider, Pete Kalmbach, as Vice-President and began to groom him to be the next CEO. In his early fifties Kalmbach had a national reputation and could easily step into the breach should something unforeseen happen. If Pete Kambach had a fault, it was his inability to be "one of the boys," to live it up and roar through life. Though a fine and honorable man, he was the antithesis of Gerry Hill. The stage had been set for office politics of the most vicious nature.

Chapter 21

BEAU GESTE

A Magnanimous Gesture

As expected, many of the company's executives resented Kalmbach. Of course the main reason for their discontent was jealousy, the realization that MacLean and Pierce had eliminated them from consideration to the top post. They closed ranks, inveigled Gerry to be their leader, and tried to force Kalmbach out. Had Gerry and his crowd been successful, I am convinced that he would have been the president, despite his age. But these men did not really give a hoot about Gerry. They were currying favor with him, trying to position themselves for future promotion at the expense of the stockholders.

Gerry fell for the sales pitch hook, line, and sinker. Personally I was appalled and did my best to stay above the fray and do my job. Though carrying little political clout, I still was one of eighteen executives in the Mass Mutual. Inevitably Gerry came to me for my support.

"Listen, Dick," he said conspiratorially. "You know what's going on. You know we are trying to oust Kalmbach. I would be grateful if you backed us up."

"I'm sorry. I really don't have the stomach for all this. There is nothing evil about the man. He's a fine actuary and a gentleman from head to toe."

"He's a prig and you know he's a prig. Can you imagine what life would be like around here with such a pompous ass at the helm?"

"Pete's not all that bad," I said. "He just doesn't like to smoke, drink, or swear. Is that all that bad?"

"Just ask the other guys. They can't stand him."

"No," I said firmly. "I'm hired to do my work, not play politics."

Gerry then said something I'll never forget.

"You really don't get it, Dick, do you? *There are times for office work and then there are times for office politics. This is a time for office politics.* You are welcome to join us at any time. But don't wait too long. You can't join the team after the game is over."

In all fairness to Gerry what transpired never affected our friendship in the slightest. The campaign against Kalmbach continued unabated. I really felt sorry for him. Here was a fair-minded decent man, a man with impeccable credentials, a man admired and respected by the Board of Directors, and what had it gotten him? To the brink of collapse, that's what. Then it happened: Alex MacLean dropped dead at the age of sixty-one. All hell broke loose. As Gerry put it, "I was seated up front with the driver and he fell off the coach."

With the exception of Gerry the plotters panicked and hastened to see Harry Pierce. They knew Pierce was the kingmaker with the Board of Directors and beseeched him to accept the CEO position rather than handing the reins over to Kalmbach. Pierce, the soul of integrity, insisted that Alex MacLean's word be honored, even in death.

"Gentlemen," Pierce said. "I have no other choice. I must recommend to the Board that Mr. Kalmbach be given the job. He has fulfilled his end of the agreement most admirably."

That was that. Pete Kalmbach was elected CEO in a matter of days. I can recall Harry Pierce and the new CEO walking into the executive lunchroom. The new CEO was oozing with gratitude.

"Thank you, Mr. Pierce," Kalmbach said loud enough for all to hear. "I can't thank you enough for the support you have given me today. I will do everything in my power to be worthy of your confidence."

Nothing much happened after that for several months, except Gerry was no longer present when questions of company policy were decided unless the group line was directly involved. Meanwhile, Kalmbach had hired a personal assistant who served as the company's executive VP. One morning this assistant came into my office unannounced and said he wanted to speak to me confidentially on a matter of great importance.

"Nothing we say can go outside of these four walls," he said. "Is that understood?"

"Yes, sir."

"The boss and I find ourselves in a delicate and uncomfortable position. After numerous talks we have reached the conclusion that it would be better for all concerned if Mr. Hill were to leave the company. His behavior just before Mr. MacLean's death had made him untrustworthy."

"Yes, I can understand that," I said. "But how do I fit into this?"

"Good question. Simply put, we want Hill out and for you to take over the company's entire group operation. You are not only the perfect man for the job but you didn't dirty your hands in this sordid affair. We are also sensitive to the fact that you and Mr. Hill are the best of friends. Were we to release Gerry, you might go too. That would be a personal loss too great for even a company like ours to sustain. What do you say?"

For a few moments I said nothing.

"I don't know what to say right now. I'm a bit stunned and need some time to mull things over. Obviously this is a life-alternating decision. I need to consult with my wife."

"I understand," he said. "I only hope you decide to accept the offer and stay with us. A man of Mr. Hill's age and ability will find work elsewhere."

Well, I was in a horrible position, a position made doubly horrible by my contempt for ambition and personal gain. Gerry was by far my best friend and had been instrumental in our coming to Springfield in the first place. Now what was I supposed to do? Stab my best buddy in the back? If I did his career would be, for all intents and purposes, destroyed. Yes, he was still relatively young but had abandoned becoming a Fellow of the Society of Actuaries years ago. Instead, he had developed a group line for the company. Then there was the question of him being branded a troublemaker in the industry. Were he to be fired, word would leak out making it virtually impossible for him to secure a position commensurate with his talents.

Marcelle and I discussed my predicament for two nights in a row.

"The easiest thing for me to do is to refuse the offer," I said. "But that would forever label me as Gerry's man, and his future with the company is flawed due to his stupid behavior."

"That leaves you one of two choices," she said. "Either you accept the job and cut Gerry loose or resign and find a job elsewhere."

"Which do you think is best?"

"That's not for me to say. I will stand behind whatever one you chose, but I will not make the decision for you."

"Well, could you at least tell me which way you are leaning?"

"No," she said with pursed lips. "That's not my place. My place is to support you. Your place is to decide: *beau geste* or no *beau geste*. It's all up to you."

I chose the *beau geste* and resigned from the Mass Mutual giving no one–not even Harry Pierce–my reason. Many, many people asked why I was leaving.

"I just don't get it," they would say. "Your future here seemed so bright and your family seemed so happy."

"The offer from the New England Life is too good for me to pass up," I lied.

The *beau geste* proved to be an exercise in futility. I was stupid not to foresee this. Pete Kambach, being aware of Gerry's slanderous remarks about his character, never could forgive him. Gerry had effectively placed an insurmountable barrier between himself and that handful of executives who determined the company's destiny. Sure, he retained his position with regards to the group line. But his job was nothing more than a glorified "Little Siberia"– limited and totally dependent on orders from "above." This was a far cry from the halcyon days when he had been the fair-haired boy with a boundless future before him. As a result, Gerry turned more and more to drink which led to his early demise, some four years shy of retirement.

PART THREE

Boston

Chapter 22

MAL VU

Badly Regarded

The CEO of the New England Life Insurance Company treated Walter Tebbits, the executive VP, like a buffoon. Walter accepted the role on the condition that he could keep his seat on the Board of Directors after retirement. I would have accepted Walter's docility if he had not reneged on a former CEO's oral agreement with me, namely I be tapped as VP and actuary in charge of group operations after meeting specific goals and objectives. Inside of five years I had done just that. My department was running like a fine Swiss timepiece, and I eagerly awaited my reward. One day Tebbits summoned me to his office.

"I have bad news for you, Dick. When I retire, a fellow Harvard MBA will become titular head of the line that you developed."

I was dumbfounded.

"I don't understand," I said. "When I took this job, I was promised I would be promoted to an executive position as long as I performed my work satisfactorily. Please tell me in what respects my work has fallen short."

"You know your work has not fallen short," he said. "The CEO just wants the other man. There is really nothing I can do."

I was furious but tried my best to contain myself.

"Well, let's go together and see the CEO. Maybe we can talk some sense into him."

"No," he said firmly. "I have already had it out with him. His decision is final."

I then made some oral attempts to meet directly with the CEO, but these too fell on deaf ears. I finally wrote a short note stating exactly why I needed to talk with him. This too was ignored. Under the circumstances I had no choice but to resign.

I have been to Boston many times since leaving the New England Life but have never attempted to contact any of my colleagues who worked there. The bitterness that I felt was so severe that I just could not bring myself to see them again. This shows just how deeply I had been hurt, for I had a reputation as a man who did not bear a grudge. Though a Christian attribute, such a character trait does not do a man any good in a world where greed and avarice abound.

A group of Johnny-come-lately Harvard MBAs at the New England Life had really played me for a sucker. They had taken control of the company's affairs with the precipitous retirement of the CEO with whom I had made a seemingly solid commitment. Indeed, I had had several other offers from other companies that promised an immediate title, but I took the more challenging job at the New England Life instead.

All this chicanery damaged me professionally. I had joined the New England Life just prior to my forty-fifth birthday. Being an expert in both life and health insurance and pensions, I was much in demand since those two fields had rapidly expanded after the end of World War II. Forced out of the New England Life in 1958 at the age of fifty, I now found myself in a more competitive environment– one in which other men now "hastened to fill the void."

Chapter 23

PEINE FORTE ET DURE

Strong and Harsh Punishment

Not everything in Springfield had been hunky-dory. For instance, health-wise Marcelle had had a hysterectomy and Gerry suffered from epilepsy. But despite these two setbacks the overall experience there had been most positive. We had a plentitude of neighborhood friends along with many families from the two insurance companies with whom I had worked. At the time I took this for granted. It was not until we moved to Waban, a small upper-middle class suburban community outside of Boston, did I realize just how great the social life in Springfield had been.

Marcelle and I bought a spacious house on Waban Avenue. Due to poor maintenance we were able to purchase the house for the bargain-basement price of twenty-nine thousand dollars. Over the next few years we invested twenty thousand dollars to make it move livable and better suited to company parties. After my resignation from the New England Life five years later, the new owners made out like bandits: paying a paltry thirty thousand dollars for "the white elephant."

Unlike her twin sister Marcelle enjoyed the company of women and had never had any trouble making friends. In Waban, however, she struggled. For instance, it took her a few years to form a bridge club, and when she did, it consisted of women from outside the neighborhood– women who held themselves above the common herd. I could never figure out what Marcelle saw in them, but this much I do know: they sure knew how to raid our liquor cabinet.

The Waban social life affected Marcelle much more than me. My work at the office took up the majority of my time and energy. I would frequently work late and upon returning home would retire early, leaving Marcelle to herself. To this day I feel guilty for not perceiving the negative effects our move to Waban had on Marcelle. In all fairness my colleagues at the New England Life lived in or near one of the great American cultural centers, hence they had less time on their hands. Yes, we soon joined the Waban Neighborhood Club and eventually became members of the prestigious Brae Burn County Club whose ranks boasted the likes of Vaughn Monroe.[18] Still, I never felt like I fit in there.

Your mother and I never really recovered from the Waban fiasco. Although our life in Springfield had its drawbacks, overall it was a much better match for us. The Springfield crowd had been genuinely cordial and sincere; the Waban crowd was not. Here we came face-to-face with the stereotypical Yankees: cold, aloof, and fixated on their petty self-interests. This did not take a long time to figure out. Indeed on our first day in Springfield the neighbors instantly came over and introduced themselves, whereas in Waban our first day passed without incident. Your mother was much to bright and clever not to notice this. And with her shyness and sensitivity she must have been cut to the quick.

I was far too busy at the office to note the change this had wrought in Marcelle. That was a terrible failure on my part. After all I had taken Marcelle to live in an alien land far from the environment where her family had provided so much gayety and fun. With her native charm and optimism Marcelle gradually made a few friends, but none could match the "bosom buddies" she had had in Springfield. She had to be very lonely.

Having acquaintances rather than friends had little effect on me since I was so absorbed with office work. Still, my neglect of Marcelle at this juncture was inexcusable. Being in her early forties when we came to Waban, Marcelle was struggling with various issues singular to her sex. At this point in our life I should have thought more of my wife and less of my career and social standing.

---

[18] American baritone singer, trumpeter, big band leader, and actor.

PART FOUR

Jacksonville

Chapter 24

COUTE QUE COUTE

Cost What It May

While my marketability had been ruined insofar as obtaining a senior executive position in a substantial life insurance company in the Northeast, there were still plenty of positions available elsewhere. After due consideration I decided to accept employment with the Gulf Life Insurance Company in Jacksonville, Florida. The Gulf Life was an established company with its stock so widely scattered that I deemed it impregnable to mergers and nefarious takeover schemes. Oh, how I underestimated the power of the Texans! But more on that later.

I chose our residence with care. Still aware of my neglect of Marcelle and the boys in Boston, I had hoped that my new job with the Gulf Life would not put so many demands upon my time. Before Marcelle had put on weight, she had enjoyed athletics, especially those that pertained to the beach. I therefore looked for a spot within reasonable driving distance to the Jacksonville beaches. We purchased a place on the St. John's River about one-third distance between Jacksonville and the beaches. We also joined the Ponte Vedre Golf Club,[19] a fine golf course with a lovely private beach for members only. I knew Marcelle would never play again, but I hoped that she would take up swimming once more. Unfortunately she did not. She was vain enough not to appear on the beach where she had previously drawn the admiring glances of onlookers. She had now become accustomed to drinking in the afternoon and had lost any desire to leave the house. From the outset she confined herself to the house and had nothing good to say about Florida or its climate. She missed the old cocktail crowd in Waban but made no attempt to form a new one.

---

[19] Nowadays this club is the home to the PGA Players Championship, one of America's premier golf events.

Chapter 25

VA ET VIENT

Coming and Going

Marcelle was not a heavy drinker. Whereas her mother consumed a fifth a day, Marcelle only drank about two-fifths a week. Still, that was enough for her to avoid becoming friendly with the other "girls" in the neighborhood. Socially Jacksonville resembled Springfield much more than Waban as far as friendliness was concerned. There was not much I could do. From the first we were wined and dined by my fellow actuaries at the company, including the president and his wife. Marcelle was fine once I got her out, but getting her out was a real chore. She had her own car so transportation was not the problem. To be closer to the beach, however, forced us to live in a more rural setting where neighbors were few and far between. Clearly I had made a mistake in over-thinking where we should live. Marcelle did have one bosom buddy nearby, Lillie Raftery.[20] But Lillie's friendship could not satisfy all her needs. Unfortunately the wives of my office associates lived several miles away on the other side of the city.

Marcelle never ceased to criticize Florida. That was particularly galling, especially when she went on and on about Waban being a veritable paradise. Here we held diametrically opposite opinions. During the seven years we lived there we attended several company conventions and actuarial meetings. We also vacationed in North Carolina and spots along the Gulf Coast, made trips to Vancouver to see her mother, and visited New England so many times that I could

---

[20] The quintessential Georgia blonde, Lillie Raftery was not only Marcelle's closest friend "on the river" but Gerry's benefactor as well. After Dick and Marcelle moved back North, "Aunt Lillie" took Gerry in her home after his epilepsy made it impossible for him to stay in the dormitories at Jacksonville University.

drive the road between there and Jacksonville blindfolded. All to no avail: Marcelle continued to detest Florida. Nonetheless, I loved Marcelle so much that whatever she did was all right with me. As far as I know, she felt the same about me. Truly she was a wonderful wife and I miss her mightily.

The Gulf Life was a great place until the Texans moved in and took it over. My duties were vital and stimulating, and I had plenty of support from top management. Nonetheless, my age showed that I had a star-crossed career dating back till the time I left Springfield.

What I liked most about the Gulf Life was working with Jack Clarke. He was the cleverest person I have ever met. With his immense intellect he could have earned recognition as a genius in any field. His thought processes amazed me. He was not only a full-fledged actuary but also a topnotch legal mind. His brilliance, however, was his undoing. All but a few business executives feel uncomfortable with a subordinate smarter than themselves. Most executives employ individuals who are dumber than they are– sometimes much, much dumber. I had noticed this early on in my career and went out of my way to hide my intelligence. To Jack's credit, he too did his best not to embarrass his corporate bosses. There were times, however, when an executive would propose such a bonehead scheme that Jack felt compelled to lay bare its folly. No amount of tact and diplomacy could mask the loss of face that came with such disclosures.

Jack was also a prodigious worker– yet another strike against him. Outside business consultants just loved him, for he could understand them easily and implement their ideas. But inside the Gulf Life he fell prey to his own brilliance. I was stunned to learn that his chief form of relaxation was science fiction. Indeed he had a formidable collection of sci-fi classics. Clearly he was a man of vision. He could see that the dominance of realism in American literature would soon be a thing of the past.

PART FIVE

Vermont

Chapter 26

EN RETRAITE

In Retirement

The first seven years of my retirement were happy ones because I was able to spend more time with Marcelle. We retired to Underhill Center, Vermont where we had a house built to our specifications some twenty miles northeast of Burlington. There, I could garden to my heart's content. We made a few close friends, most notably the artists Roy and Lorraine Kennedy. These friends satisfied our need for companionship, which had become narrowed due to our advanced age. Marcelle and my lifestyles remained quite different. She continued to drink two-fifths a week, whereas I limited myself to one. I got up at 7 a.m. and gardened or wrote until noon. Then Marcelle would get up, and we would go out to eat at Joe's, a local fast food joint that served delicious hot dogs and pizza. After that, we would just diddle around till dinnertime. Then Marcelle would prepare a superb dinner befitting her French Canadian heritage. By then I had consumed my quota of spirits. Marcelle, however, deferred eating until later choosing instead to drink before eating. Afterwards we watched TV till I fell asleep on the divan around 9 p.m. Marcelle, on the other hand, rarely went to bed before midnight.

I never tired of Marcelle's company. Our friends would joke about our different routines, but they suited us fine until I had a prostatectomy with serious complications. After my lengthy convalescence on a road trip across the United States, Marcelle mentioned a lump on her breast. I immediately stopped in Phoenix, Arizona where the doctors there diagnosed breast cancer. I will not dwell on the grizzly details that led up to her death years later. You are all too familiar with them.[21] After Marcelle died, I moved to Central

---

[21] See Appendix III

Park Village in Orlando, Florida where I am composing this epistle. My life here is a lonely one, but I still find it most instructive. Old age is a part of living. If the Creator has seen fit for me to experience it, so be it.

In Vermont I started to fool around with writing during the mornings when Marcelle was asleep. I did not have a clear idea about my subject. At first I had grandiose plans for writing a multivolume work on Man but have now decided to restrict myself to the material contained in this epistle. Essentially it describes my seeking to determine the purpose for which my spirit was created in accordance with the lights with which I have been endowed.

During the Great Depression I had become engrossed with the crumbling economic systems throughout the world. Intellectually I was literally "born again" in an economic and historic sense. Deeply suspicious of propaganda, I became terribly selective in who and what I read. As a result, I neglected my actuarial studies and focused solely on the plight of mankind.

I read into the wee hours of the night. I was far too conscientious to let my reading interfere with my office responsibilities. I therefore redoubled my work during the day so I could pursue my self-studies at night. Still, I could not resist talking about world affairs with several of my close friends who had also been shaken from their complacency. I soon became known as a savant in economic and political matters. This did not endear me with the Sun Life management who could not and would not continence any criticism of the status quo. Of all the actuarial men there, I was the only one to stray from the strait and narrow path that led to becoming a fellow in the Society of Actuaries. Though this would later come back to haunt me, I never regretted my decision.

As my knowledge of economics increased, I began to question whether or not communism, specifically Russian communism, had any validity. Sure, communism looked good on paper, but some of the basic doctrines posed serious philosophic problems. Marx's Labor Theory of Value, for instance, sounded good. One could argue that the only value of any commodity was the work put into it. But was that always true? What if you had two identical oilrigs in the same locale and at the same depth–the first a gusher and the second dry as a bone? Wouldn't the gusher be more valuable with the same amount of labor? On the other hand, fascism–being essentially the dictatorship of the middle class–was in every respect despicable. In a word I could not embrace either system over the slow-plodding Western democracies. With great eloquence and passion I turned down membership in the Canadian Communist Party time and time again. It was simply not my cup of tea.

The transition away from communism and towards democracy was a long and arduous one with my courtship of Marcelle playing a significant role. As my interest in her rose, my fascination with the state of affairs in Russia and Germany took a nosedive. Being invited to the birthday party of the twins on June 12, 1933 was really the beginning of the end of my days as a political activist, though I did not know it the time. Subsequently my political thought was more aligned with Winston Churchill than Karl Marx, to wit *"Many forms of Government have been tried and will be tried in this world of sin and woe. No one pretends that democracy is perfect or all-wise. Indeed, it has been said that democracy is the worst form of government except all those other forms that have been tried from time to time."*

Unfortunately my foray into politics and economics had rendered me "snake bit" as Southerners are wont to say. My readings had trained me to spot political propaganda a mile away, especially the political propaganda of the business establishment. This I could not and would not remove from my consciousness. Reading had always been the love of my life and I would never give it up. I therefore became a male Cassandra, incessantly predicting events well in advance of their occurrence. This would often baffle my business associates. Lacking any depth in current events, they saw me as a bit of a nut, someone who belonged and yet who did not belong. Marcelle was the only one in my social circle who seemed to understand me, to be sincerely interested in what I said. But Marcelle was an audience of one. My father, on the other hand, took a more practical approach. "That is all very well, Dick" he would often say, "but what can you do about it?" Of course that was true. Still, I could not help myself. My mind demanded analysis and understanding on a continual basis. It was as if I had a mental addiction.

Ultimately I arrived at a fundamental conclusion: mankind's ills emanated from the psyches of humans themselves. From that point onward, though continuing to read extensively, I held out no hope of finding a cause that would generate a positive outcome. I was in this state of mind when Jeanne invited me to the twins twenty-first birthday party in the spring of 1933. Having experienced four years of the Great Depression, I was no longer the naïve, insensitive clod of yore. I had now acquired a deep interest in humans and their woes, and I would forever after read books that endeavored to better the human condition. Of course, this made me an oddball in the business world since my values did not jive with capitalistic "success." Apart from that, I was ripe for the picking when Marcelle welcomed me warmly at her party. She quickly became the center of my life, and I wooed her accordingly.

PART SIX

Orlando

Chapter 27

LE COEUR A SES RAISONS QUE LA RAISON NE CONNAIT POINT

The Heart Has Its Reasons That Reason Knows Nothing Of

At no time did my love for Marcelle waver. She proved to be my one true love. I am far from sure that this was reciprocated, but she never gave me cause to believe it was not. That was sufficient to render anything unfavorable about our marriage inconsequential. In retrospect, she provided me with a most happy life for which I will be forever grateful.

In most love affairs there is the one who loves with the other being satisfied to be loved. In my case I was the former, and Marcelle was the latter. I was therefore delighted, in a bittersweet way, when from her deathbed she whispered, "My darling, I love you with all my heart."

FINIS

APPENDIX I

Thoughts on a Foursome:
Golf in Val-Morin Circa 1931[22]

Marineval is situated in the Aurent Mountains. It is now a popular summer resort and, although it was feared at the beginning that its charms might be usurped by undesirables, such has been the influence of the church authorities that now it is only frequented by those who by means of their well-funded credit are able to secure that exclusiveness which enhances their egoism and in their own minds sets them above the ordinary.

What attracted me at first was probably that the scenery reminded me of my own native country of Newland. I have gone there summer after summer and have found its restful quiet and wholesome air a great tonic to the mind as well as to the body.

As one dips over the hill that makes its southern entrance to the Vale –as it is called–one can see its whole beauty stretched out as a picture. I have often stopped at this point and contemplated the whole scene. The valley is not symmetrical and this gives it a peculiar fascination for across from the spot the hills rise in tiers – topped by the residences of those who through fortunes fancy, have been enabled to secure the much-desired viewpoints. It appears at first glance that there should be corresponding tiers on this side and one's glance tends to seek for them causing one to turn again to study the landscape to find why this is not so. In the bottom of the Vale, surrounded by the numerous varicolored boathouses each carrying the flag designating the club is Lake Mond. The whole ensemble appears as a jewel with the appropriate setting, each of whose component parts appear as if it were definitely designed to harmonize with the others. Stretching around the lake and on this side of it looking from the south

---

[22] This dated sketch was found amongst my father's papers. Though of little literary value, it depicts a recreational culture and a sporting world that is gone forever.

one can see the now-famous golf course. Even those who have not played the game have heard of its exclusiveness and its spacious clubhouse. The latter lies on our left, its verandah overlooking the ninth and eighteenth greens. To sit on this verandah with a well-drawing pipe and behold the golfers as they play onto the greens is a pleasant way to spend a philosophic hour. Very interesting is it to note the various types and their reactions to the results of their shots.

One June morning I was sitting here in company of the senior professional, Mr. Land. He was telling me of some games in which he had played, and, like any other golfer, of the marvelous and lucky recoveries he had made: shots from the rough and shots from the bunkers, together with humorous incidents which showed the game to be not without its lighter moments despite the serious demeanor of many of its devotees.

As we were talking, a car drove up to the entrance and Mr. Land leaving me for other duties advised me that if I was looking for something interesting I could do no better than to notice the foursome, which was now arriving. It was evidently a holiday and Mr. Worth[23] had let his chauffeur off for the day for he was driving his own car. Of the foursome three of them I was acquainted with but I was quite intimate with Mr. Yard.[24] The other two were Mr. Mas[25] and Mr. Ore.[26] Mr. Worth had recently purchased an estate in the region and this foursome had evidently come up to spend a few days. When I said that it was "an interesting foursome," I meant it apart from the game of golf.

Mr. Mas is known as a free and advanced thinker. We can all remember his arguments against the so-called capitalistic system and how it should be superseded by other schemes depending on the idealistic idea that everything should be shared in common. I fancy that when he hits a ball long and far into the rough that it gives some indication of what he is desirous of doing to a capitalist. I do not think, however, that he has any animosity towards such personally. Yard had told me that while Mas has a definite superiority complex, it never shows itself prominently and that he is continually by smaller acts repressing its manifestation.

---

[23] Jack Ashworth
[24] "Slim" Hillyard
[25] William R. Christmas
[26] Art Moore

Mr. Ore is the well-known mathematician connected with the Moon Life Insurance Company[27] whose crest is the moonshine on a placid sheet of water. Though a conservative and the most brilliant of the foursome in the realm of scholastic attainments, Mr. Ore is not one to impose his ideas upon others. He has a materialistic view of world in general and is not much concerned with the views of Mr. Mas, except as they interfere with his own. I hear through Yard that Ore's son is making a name for himself at the University of Mount Gill[28] as his father did.

Mr. Worth is a self-made man. It is rumored that he helped on the building of his residence about three miles from here. According to Yard, Worth enjoys walking around his estate no matter how hot it may be or how plentiful the flies. He does not travel as far along the road of radicalism as Mas. Instead he believes in the established order tempered by the introduction of Christian ethics into business. Yard has informed me that Mas and Worth have argued at length on this point and that he, Yard, has managed to keep the argument balanced.

Mr. Yard–the last of the foursome–is, as I have intimated, the best known to me. While some of my deductions concerning the rest of the foursome may be erroneous, I am quite certain when it comes to Yard, the only one of the foursome, never to have married. Some have claimed that this has greatly affected his life, but this I do not believe. He has told me on occasions that women were too much in evidence in business and political life, in his opinion, and that their place was in the home. This of course is evidence of his non-progressive mind, his unwillingness to move far from the accepted view of things. Yard at times strikes me as peculiar. Imaginative and dreamy, he does not see the world as it is. He has confided that even when walking the street he may be oblivious of everything– lost completely in the creations of his own imagination. He strives after the ideal and consequently misses the gifts of the present. Mr. Arnes,[29] the famous critic and master of irony, accuses Yard of being "intellectually dishonest"– whatever that means. But I do not think there is anything dishonest about him in the ordinary sense of the word. He is probably a bit of a hypocrite, but his beliefs are all focused in his arguments. With regards to Mas' stance on world systems, Yard does not agree, believing that what the people

---
[27] The Sun Life Insurance Company of Montreal, Canada.
[28] McGill University
[29] Bill Barnes

desire in the mass will ultimately come forward. Arnes in his book, *The Effect of the Sunday School on the Child Mind*, also ridicules Mas' idea saying that people have no will. Yard, however, say that Arnes writes books only for commercial gain and must learn to say something.

With these few remarks on each – very sketchy at best – you will perceive that it was an interesting foursome. They paired Ore and Yard versus Mas and Worth. I noticed as they teed off that they all used "Gofar" balls, advocated by Arnes in his book, *Practicing on the Common*.

All four men got good drives off the first tee with the exception of Mas who topped his ball for a mere two hundred yards. I would have liked to follow them around and watched their play, but with the exception of a few commonplace remarks I had to let them go. It was evidently a very close game and when they later arrived on the 18th green I noticed that Ore was in great glee– evidently he had had a good play. I later learned that he had sunk his approach from 150 yards out although he did not have the pleasure of displaying it as the others were selfishly attempting to play their own balls. Worth appeared very cynical as if it didn't matter what he did or didn't do next. I noticed Yard had kept score and I was mean enough to remember Arnes's criticism of hypocrisy. Mas evidently had played the best game but had been discounted by Yard's insisting on handicapping him. I later heard that Yard had moments of play in which he forgot his surroundings and in one particular bunker was unable to use his customary nonchalance.

The outcome of the conversation held by this foursome as they went around the course, I understand, is to be gathered together by Arnes and published under the title *The Truth Will Out* or *The Coming Struggle for Pre-eminence*.

The next installment will give a hole-by-hole account of the play as told to me by Yard.

APPENDIX II

Constitution:
League for Intellectual Advancement (1934)[30]

Preamble

WHEREAS there exists a group of young people desirous of making mutual contribution of talents and brains for the cultural improvement of the individuals of the group;

NOW this group convenes this twentieth day of February Anno Domini one thousand nine hundred and thirty-four for the adoption of the following constitution and by-laws.

Constitution

Article 1 – NAME

This group with all branches, which hereafter may be formed, shall be known as the LEAGUE FOR INTELLECTUAL ADVANCEMENT. Each branch shall be allotted a number upon its affiliation being recognized, this original group to be designated Branch Number One.

Articles 2 – OBJECTS

The objects of this League shall be to promote, stimulate, and foster the thoughts of its members towards a fuller and more conscious understanding of their duties, obligations, and opportunities as members of the human race but cultural self-improvement and mutual

---

[30] This Constitution was enacted at the first meeting of The League for Intellectual Advancement on February 20, 1934. The members of the League so impressed the Communist Party of Canada that they were approached and asked to become party members on a number of occasions. A few actually accepted much to the distress of William Richard Christmas.

contribution of talents and brains for the training of the members in making a critical and sympathetic study of the ideals and institutions on which the social orders are constructed, the ideas which brought them forth, the needs they are expected to meet, the results of their workings on the communities and the possibility of their betterment. The League shall be non-sectarian and without political affiliation. Harmony with frankness and co-operation with candor on the part of all members are essentials to the achievement of the objects of the League.

In keeping with the aims of the League there shall exist no restrictions upon the conduct of the individual members at regular meetings except that it shall be the privilege of any member to raise the question of another member's conduct on a point of order and, if sustained, such member shall be obliged to desist from such conduct. Further, while the objects of the League are to be fostered, the League can in no way be held responsible for the actions or conduct of the members other than at the meetings of the organization.

Article 3 – MEMBERSHIP

SECTION 1: The membership of each branch of the League shall be limited to young people, none of whom shall be less than twenty-one or more than thirty-five years of age upon admittance to the branch.

SECTION 2: Upon attainment of age forty, members shall be granted the privilege of retaining affiliation with their respective branches as associate members without active or voting power but shall be entitled to free participating in debate.

SECTION 3: Each branch shall be limited to a membership of twelve, with eight considered the most desirable number, while six is the minimum with which a branch can retain its affiliation. It is provided, however, that upon the membership of a branch reaching a number less than six, that branch shall continue to be affiliated for a period of two months before losing its connection with the League.

SECTION 4: Branches may be formed by the division of existing branches of twelve members into separate branches of six members each, which may be augmented by the acquisition of new members as hereinafter provided, but only within the limits of Section 3 of the Article; except that Branch Number One shall not be privileged so to divide, although members can resign from it to form new branches, providing the membership of said Branch Number One is at no time less than eight.

SECTION 5: A branch may also be formed by at least six interested young people applying to any recognized branch for affiliation with the League. In such an event the recognized branch will appoint three delegates of whom two must be present at each of the meetings of the new branch (which will only be recognized by the League following its holding four regular weekly meetings) for a period of four months. Such delegates will act in a purely advisory capacity, interpreting the Constitution of the League, its aims, and ideals. They shall be without active or voting power in such meetings. A member to be eligible at act as a delegate shall be required to have been a member of the League for a period of not less than six months.

SECTION 6: Applicants for membership in any branch shall be considered after they have attended at least two regular meetings of such branch as guests of members and have submitted completed Application for Membership forms. Each applicant shall be recommended by at least one regular member, in good standing, and maybe admitted to such branch by a majority vote of the membership.

SECTION 7: A member, in good standing with any recognized branch, may transfer his membership to any other branch providing his or her desire to transfer has been intimated in writing to the first branch at least two weeks prior to the time of such transfer becoming effective, and further, providing the second branch by a majority vote of its membership accepts him or her as a member. There shall be no probationary period.

Article 4 – OFFICERS

SECTION 1: By lot cast at each regular meeting of each branch there shall be selected a chairman who shall officiate for the duration of the meeting and any adjournments thereof, except that only those who have not so acted shall be included in the casting of lots until all members shall have so acted; then reversion to general casting shall be made and the procedure repeated as often as may be necessary. A further exception shall be that no speaker or reviewer of the meeting shall be included in the casting of lots for the chairmanship regardless of other regulations.

SECTION 2: There shall be a secretary-treasurer elected upon the formation, and upon each anniversary of the formation, of each branch. The term of office shall be one year, commencing upon election. The holder shall not be eligible for re-election until an interval of at least one term has occurred.

SECTION: 3: By lot there shall be selected by each branch one delegate who, in company with the secretary-treasurer of that branch, shall attend the General Meeting, as provided for in Article 6, Section 3, except that only those who have not so acted shall be included in the casting of lots until all members shall have so acted. A further exception shall be that the secretary-treasurer shall not be included in the casting of lots.

SECTION 4: By lot at each General Meeting there shall be selected a chairman who shall officiate for the duration of the meeting and any adjournment thereof, except that the secretary-treasurer of Branch Number One shall not be included in the casting of lots.

SECTION 5: The secretary of each General Meeting shall be the then current incumbent of the secretary-treasurership of Branch Number One.

SECTION 6: There shall be a Programme Committee of three members elected upon the formation of each branch. The term of office shall be six months, commencing upon elections. The members of this Committee shall not be eligible for re-election until an interval of at least one term has occurred. Except for the first Committee so elected, Elections shall take place at least three weeks prior to the expiry date of the term of each currently active Committee.

Article 5 – DUTIES OF OFFICERS

SECTION 1: It shall be the duty of each chairman, in his or her turn, to call the meeting to order at the hour to which it stands adjourned; to enforce a rigid observance of the Constitution of the League and the by-laws, rules and regulations of the branch; to provide over all debates; and otherwise to see to the proper conduct of the meeting held under his or her membership.

SECTION 2: It shall be the duty of the secretary-treasurer to keep a record of the deliberations and business proceedings of the branch; to manage its funds; to give a report upon his or her management when so requested by a majority vote of the branch; and to attend all General

Meetings held during his or her tenure of office and to report thereon to the branch at its next regular meeting following each General Meeting.

SECTION 3: It shall be the duty of each delegate to a General Meeting conscientiously, to the best of his or her ability, to represent the branch to which he or she belongs and to report in conjunction with he secretary-treasurer of his of her branch upon deliberations of such General Meeting to his or her branch at its first regular meeting following the General Meeting.

SECTION 4: It shall be the duty of the chairman of each General Meeting to call such meeting to order at the hour to which it stands adjourned; to enforce a rigid observance of the Constitution of the League and of all by-laws, rules, and regulations affecting General Meetings; to preside over all debates; and to see, otherwise, to the proper conduct of such meeting.

SECTION 5: It shall be the duty of the Secretary of General Meetings to keep a record or the deliberations and business proceedings of said General Meetings; to notify all branches of pertinent matters; and to act generally in the capacity of liaison officer for the League.

SECTION 6: It shall be the duty of the Programme Committee to submit to the branch a programme of topics for study, of books for review or of such pertinent matters as, in its opinion, warrant attention and consideration, which programme shall require to be approved by the majority of the members of the branch before becoming a course for study and discussion. The casting of lots will determine that distribution of topics that form the programme. Only those who have not participated in the programme shall be included in the casting of lots until all members have been allotted a portion of the programme; then reversion to general casting shall be made and the procedure repeated as often as may be necessary.

Article 6 – MEETINGS

SECTION 1: Each branch shall assemble one evening in each week, unless otherwise ordered, for the promotion of the objects of the League and the transaction of the business of the branch.

SECTION 2: The first regular weekly meeting of each branch in the months of January, March, May, July, September, and November of each year shall be designated for discussion of topics of general interest. At such meetings each branch shall receive as guests not fewer than two nor more than three members of some other branch, except that no member of the second branch shall act as a guest upon two consecutive occasions.

SECTION 3: Upon the first Saturday evening of each of the months of March, September, and December of each year there shall convene the secretary-treasurers of all branches together with the delegates designated in Article 4, Section 3, to form a General Meeting of the League for discussions of business affecting the League as a whole and for promotion of harmonious relations between branches. Included in the business of any such General Meeting shall be the arrangements for exchange of visitors, as described in the preceding sections, and arrangements for the securing of a complete vote of the members of the League, when required, upon subjects pertinent to the League as a whole.

Article 7 – QUORUM

SECTION 1: At any meeting of a branch a majority of its membership shall constitute a quorum.

SECTION 2: At any General Meeting of the League of those eligible to attend shall constitute a quorum.

Article 8 - ABSENTEE VOTE

No member of any branch shall be considered to have resigned (except as hereinafter provided) unless his or her resignation be submitted in writing two weeks prior to the date of such resignation becoming effective. Non-attendance at two consecutive, regular meetings of his or her branch, except in the case of illness or advice of expected absence, shall be considered evidence of resignation. Resignation of a member of any branch, for any other reason whatsoever, can be requested only upon majority vote of the membership of his or her branch.

Article 9 – ABSENTEE VOTE

In the event of the absence of a member of any branch from a regular meeting of that branch any member present may call for the appointment of a committee of two members for the purpose of (1) acquainting the absentee with the phrasing of any motion or motions and the debate thereon, and (2) securing such absentee's vote. In such an event no decision can be said to have been made by the branch until all such absentees' vote have been received and recorded at the next meeting of the branch when the results of the voting at the previous meeting and the voting of absentee or absentees shall be considered jointly.

Article 10 – AMENDMENTS

No addition, alteration, or amendment can be made to this Constitution. Neither can any part of it is repealed without a three-quarter vote of the League, and two weeks' previous notice, in writing, to the Secretary of General Meetings.

LEAGUE FOR INTELLECTUAL ADVANCEMENT

BRANCH NUMBER ONE
By-laws

Article 1 - MEETINGS

SECTION 1: This branch shall assemble Tuesday evening in each week, unless otherwise ordered, for the promotion of the objects of the League and the transaction of business of the Branch.

SECTION 2: The hour of the meeting shall be eight o'clock p.m.

APPENDIX III

January 18, 1985

Report to Dr. Reardon: Written 10:30 a.m.[31]

Marcelle's condition last night was changed to the extent she couldn't settle down to sleep for the night until 2:00 a.m.

She awakened about 5:00 a.m. complaining of a feeling of general malaise and of being in considerable pain. On ingesting a Tylenol with codeine pill and a compazine pill she tried to settle down but found little if any relief. She started crying and all she would say was "I feel rotten and sore all over." She claimed the pain was severe but bearable; however, her entire general bodily discomfort was a different matter. She wanted to know if my mother had ever felt like this and I could truthfully answer "no."

From then on her discomfort was so great that she became restless to the extent that she could not lie down, sit up, or stand up except for a moment at a time.

Between intermittent crying she would say: "I wish God would take me" or "I have nothing to look forward to." She actually was distraught for a considerable length of time for the first time. Her mood has become one of deep despondency.

I was not with her after 10:00 p.m. last night as Gerry and I spell each other in caring for her. Around midnight she broke down for a spell and said to him, "If I continue like this, I don't think life is worth living." This sentiment she reiterated to him about 10:00 a.m. this morning.

---

[31] Dick wrote this report three weeks before Marcelle's death.